VENTRILOQUISM

VENTRILOQUISM

Darryl Hutton

STERLING
PUBLISHING CO., INC.   NEW YORK

I dedicate this book to my most successful students of ventriloquism, Lawrence Clayton & Richie Lee, Steven Wyard & Charlie, Brian Hunter & Danny

Adapted from the book "Modern Ventriloquism" © 1974 by Darryl J. P. Hutton, published in Great Britain by Kaye & Ward Ltd., London.

Copyright © 1975 by Darryl Hutton
Published by Sterling Publishing Co., Inc.
Two Park Avenue, New York, N.Y. 10016
Distributed in Australia by Oak Tree Press Co., Ltd.
P.O. Box K514 Haymarket, Sydney 2000, N.S.W.
Distributed in the United Kingdom by Blandford Press
Link House, West Street, Poole, Dorset BH15 1LL, England
Distributed in Canada by Oak Tree Press Ltd.
% Canadian Manda Group, 215 Lakeshore Boulevard East
Toronto, Ontario M5A 3W9
Manufactured in the United States of America
All rights reserved
Library of Congress Catalog Card No.: 75-14508
Sterling ISBN 0-8069-7022-7 Trade
                    7023-5 Library
                    7670-5 Paper
First paperback printing 1982

Contents

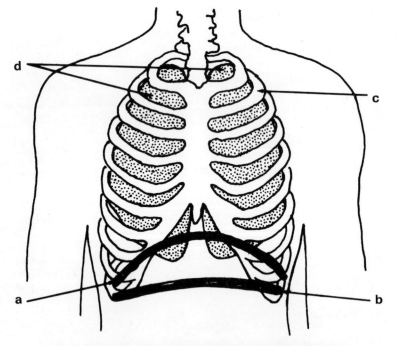

Illus. 1. Diaphragm (see pages 9, 10-15).
  a. Diaphragm is raised when you breathe out.
  b. Diaphragm is lowered when you breathe in.
  c. Rib Cage
  d. Lungs

Before You Begin

VENTRILOQUISM, on the surface, seems only to entertain, amuse and mystify, but deep down there is a strange capacity for arousing sympathy or compassion within an audience. This feeling arises out of our ability to identify with another person, who is experiencing a situation comparable to one we have known. How is this sympathy aroused during a ventriloquial performance? What is the *nature* of this feeling? What *effect* does this have upon the viewing audience?

Since the beginning of time people have tended to rebel against symbols of power and authority. When the ventriloquist's small partner is reprimanded for some misdemeanor, compassion is aroused in the audience, as they too have parents, bosses and other superiors, who sometimes seem impossible to defy.

Thus the audience identifies with this "blockhead" and "sees" and "hears" him as a real person. Since the "living doll" has evoked these feelings in the audience, it is accepted as a personality and not merely a block of wood.

For the same reason, ventriloquism was an ancient tool of communication, used by priests to animate their pagan statues, in order to enlist a large following. Some churchmen and policemen as well as entertainers in the USA use ventriloquism as a means of effectively communicating their message to a compassionately responsive audience. The educational value of ventriloquism remains to be fully exploited. As a schoolroom tool, ventriloquism could be extremely useful in engaging the attention of the young.

Ventriloquism could be a more effective and dynamic tool of communication in fields such as speech correction and sales promotion, if more creative people would tap its potentialities. I believe any ventriloquist who has a deep love for his art should and will endeavor to attract others to it so as to improve its quality and potential in such communication, quite apart from its function as an entertainment medium of a high order.

In this book, you will learn how to master the art of ventriloquism as a form of entertainment—how to use your vocal organs in such a way as to seem to "throw" your voice, how to make simple puppets and how to use patter and dialogue, lighting, sound and magic in such a way as to make an audience believe that there are *two* people on the stage—a dummy comic and a human straight man. Ventriloquism is a performing art—one that relates to puppetry, Shakespearean clowns, Laurel and Hardy, stand-up comics and conjuring.

1. What Is Ventriloquism?

VENTRILOQUISM is the art of speaking without moving the lips, so that you create an illusion of the voice coming from another source. It was first used in ancient Greek and Chinese temple rituals. One of the first known ventriloquists was the Greek philosopher, Euricles. As a form of entertainment, it has progressed from the ventriloquists who used elaborate stage settings and a whole company of figures in their acts, to today's routines which, geared for speed, usually only require one dummy and a short dialogue.

Strange as it may seem, some people believe that the dummy is really talking. You create this illusion partly by the fact that the human ear cannot always exactly pinpoint the location of a sound. You can prove this yourself by blindfolding a person and asking him to sit in the center of a large room. Then move quietly to different parts of the room and see if he can guess where the sound is coming from.

Another reason for this misconception is that the ventriloquist voice, if made correctly, is very diffuse. If the manipulation of the dummy is natural and well timed, it will attract the audience's attention away from the ventriloquist most of the time.

Contrary to popular belief, the ventriloquist is not speaking from the stomach. The voice is produced by air passing through the vocal cords in the voice box, and the sound is brought up to the front of the mouth to make it as clear and crisp as possible. Slight pressure from the diaphragm helps to push the air through the vocal cords and this may be why the idea of speaking from the stomach originated.

The three basic fundamentals of ventriloquism are: speaking without moving the lips, producing a ventriloquist voice that is different from your own and, finally, the lifelike and precisely timed manipulation of the dummy. Only when you have mastered these aspects can you put the trimmings on your act.

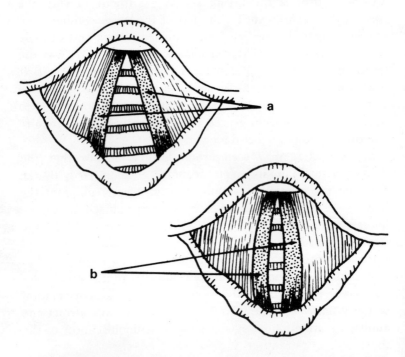

Illus. 2. The Larynx
    a. When one is breathing, but not talking or singing, the vocal cords are far apart, as in top diagram.
    b. When one is speaking, the vocal cords are closer together, forming a slit-like opening. When the diaphragm exerts pressure on the lungs, air is forced through the slit, causing the cords to vibrate and producing sound.

2. Fundamentals of the Ventriloquist Voice

BEFORE you can begin to practice the dummy voice you must master some basic techniques. First, you must be able to speak clearly *with* lip movement before you can hope to speak without it. Second, you must have control over your lip and tongue muscles. And, third, you must be able to breathe correctly so that you can produce a resonating dummy voice.

The following exercises have been designed to improve these three aspects and should be practiced carefully before moving on to the next stage.

Speaking clearly

These exercises will strengthen the muscles of your lips and jaw and so enable you to gain more control over them. Pronounce each sound very distinctly, stretching your lips.

1. he-ah-oh, he-ah-oh, he-ah-oh, he-ah-oh, he-ah-oh, he-ah-oh.
2. ah-oh-he, ah-oh-he, ah-oh-he, ah-oh-he, ah-oh-he, ah-oh-he.
3. he-who, he-who, he-who, he-who, he-who, he-who, he-who.
4. who-he, who-he, who-he, who-he, who-he, who-he, who-he.
5. he-he-who-who, he-he-who-who, he-he-who-who, he-he-who-who.

6. Repeat all the exercises with lip movement but without any sound.

Make the next sounds with expression so that your lips really stretch.

7. oh-ah! oh-ah! oh-ah! oh-ah! oh-ah!

8. ah-oh! ah-oh! ah-oh! ah-oh! ah-oh!

It is important that the dummy voice should have a resonating or vibrating quality. The exercises below should enable you to feel a vibrating sensation in your head and nasal resonating chambers (look at the picture of the organs of speech on page 10).

9. err-err-err-err-zzzzzzzzzzzzzzzzz-zod-zod-zod-zod.

err-err-err-err-zzzzzzzzzzzzzzzzz-zod-zod-zod-zod.

This last exercise will help to improve the resonating qualities of your voice. Try to *sing* it.

10. mmmmmmmmmm-ooooooooo-mmmmmmmmmm
mmmmmmmmmm-eeeeeeeeee- mmmmmmmmmm
mmmmmmmmmm-aaaaaaaaaa- mmmmmmmmmm
mmmmmmmmmm-iiiiiiiii- mmmmmmmmmm
mmmmmmmmmm-yyyyyyyyyy- mmmmmmmmmm
mmmmmmmmmm-uuuuuuuuuu- mmmmmmmmmm
nnnnnnnnnnn-gggggggggg- nnnnnnggggggg
laaaaaaaaaabambambam- aaaaaaaa-mmmm

These should be practiced in front of a mirror for at least 10 minutes. It is better to practice in short 5- to 10-minute intervals so that you will not overexert or strain your vocal cords.

Exercises to free the tongue

If you practice these exercises to strengthen the muscles of the lips and tongue for about 10 minutes a day, you should be able to speak without moving your lips in 3 or 4 weeks. But remember only to practice for short periods at a time to avoid straining the muscles of the tongue and jaw. A 5-minute practice session with rest periods is much better than one of a longer duration.

1. Make a clicking sound with the tongue by drawing it backwards along the hard palate.
2. Take a deep breath and expel the air out quickly so that the tongue vibrates.
3. Move the tongue around in circles in front of your teeth, 8 times clockwise and 8 times counterclockwise.
4. Bite the tip of the tongue about 8 times.
5. Try to swallow your tongue about 8 times.
6. Stretch the upper lip over the lower lip 8 times and then stretch the lower lip over the upper.
7. Twist your facial muscles and make a pout. Hold the facial muscles in the pout for the count of 5 and then relax.
8. Open your mouth wide and push the tip of the tongue against the back of the top teeth. Count to 4, pushing a little harder each time. Then let your jaw and tongue relax.
9. Stick out your tongue a little. As you count to 4, stick it out a little more each time. Let the muscles of your tongue relax.
10. Make a trough with your tongue and then stick it out 6 times.

Try to say these words in front of a mirror without moving your lips:

she, train, town, talk, guess, next, test, sack,

share, next, he, they, store, and, thing, there.

How to breathe (see Illus. 1, p. 6)

Health experts have claimed that the average person breathes only a third of the air required for full health and power. They only inhale air in the top part of their lungs and so are "shallow breathers." Try this test to see if you are a shallow breather:

1. Put your right hand on your chest, about 3 inches below your shoulder. Then put your left hand on your chest, about 3 inches below the right hand.
2. Breathe in naturally. Hold your breath for about 2 seconds and then exhale through your nose.
3. If the upper right hand moves in more than the lower left hand, you are a shallow breather and must correct this before trying the dummy voice.

Steps to correct breathing

1. Place your hands on your chest and take a deep breath. Your chest will expand.
2. Now exhale slowly, trying to keep the chest in an expanded position at the top. Try not to raise your shoulders while doing this. When you are exhaling, the muscles in front of your stomach and your lower ribs tend to contract or move inward.
3. Say an extended s-s-s-s-s-s-s-sound with your hand flat on your stomach. Can you feel the diaphragm muscles of your stomach contracting?

Exercise 1

Stand with your right foot forward and your hands straight out at your sides. Then, breathe in through your nose. Balance the weight of your body on your right foot as you breathe in. After inhaling as much air as your lungs can hold, bring your weight back on to your left foot, dropping your hands to your sides and slowly letting air out during the movement. Do this exercise evenly and slowly.

Exercise 2 (exhaling)

To let the air out you simply relax and the air will escape

as the muscles attached to the rib cage contract and lower, pushing the air out.

Next place your feet about 12 inches apart. Rest your hands gently on your diaphragm. Take a deep breath *slowly,* taking in as much air as you can. Then bend forward and say the word b—a—n—k—s in a stretched out manner as you exhale. Do this exercise several times with different words, such as:

(a) Good evening, Stanley   (b) Hello there.

Exercise 3 (for relaxation)

1. Stand up straight, feet apart, chest up and stomach in.
2. Take a slow, deep breath.
3. As you exhale, let your mouth fall wide open. At the same time let your head fall forward until your chin rests upon your chest. Then twist your neck to the left and right with your chin still resting upon your chest. Repeat this 6 times.

Mouth position in ventriloquism

The next step is to practice the ventriloquist's mouth position, or the position of your lips when you are speaking for the dummy, so that it looks natural and so that you can change from your voice to the dummy's quickly.

When you are speaking for the dummy, your teeth should be about a quarter of an inch apart, and your lips slightly open in a natural position. Practice this in front of a mirror so that it does not feel or look forced. Another method of mouth positioning is to smile with teeth showing.

Say these words in your own voice and then assume the ventriloquist's mouth position and say them again without any lip movement: lady; she; city; yes sir; are you going today?

Practice changing back and forth quickly.

3. Making the Voice

The beginner's alphabet

When you have mastered the first steps, you can begin to practice the sounds for the dummy's voice. The beginner's alphabet omits the letters which are hard to say with the lips apart. Repeat the letters in the ventriloquist's position.

a c d e g h i j k l n o q r s t u x y z

Practice the alphabet in front of the mirror and speed up as you go along. Repeat it over and over again *until your lips don't move*. If you practice for between 15 minutes and half an hour, you will notice a definite improvement.

In order to keep the jaw rigid and enable the tip of the tongue to move more freely, you should put your thumb and forefinger together and place them between your teeth, about a quarter of an inch into your mouth. Practice the alphabet like this and use the same method for all the hard sounds you will be learning later. The sounds will seem muffled but when you take your fingers out of your mouth, the ventriloquist voice will eventually become very clear.

How to make the dummy voice

The basis for the ventriloquist voice is a resonating, partially nasal tone. The following points are in step form to help you produce the voice as quickly as possible.

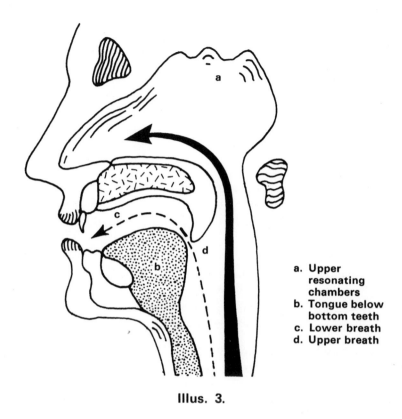

a. Upper
   resonating
   chambers
b. Tongue below
   bottom teeth
c. Lower breath
d. Upper breath

Illus. 3.

1. Say the letter "e" as in "lean" and push with your diaphragm muscles as you say it. If you push firmly enough, more of the air will be directed into the nasal passages.
2. The tongue should push firmly on the ridge just below the bottom teeth at the back (see Illus. 3).
3. Take a deep breath and elongate the "eeee" sound.

4. Try to do this buzzing "eeee" tone for 10 seconds and then try to lengthen it to 25 seconds by the end of the first week.
5. Say the beginner's alphabet in the "eeee" or buzz tone without moving your lips. Don't forget to use a mirror for this. The extended partial nasal tone is the basis for the ventriloquist voice.
6. Try to get the sounds as clear as possible by moving the tip of your tongue inside your mouth and bringing the sound up to the front of the mouth.

The Drone will give the dummy voice a vibrating quality.
1. Place the tip of your tongue behind your bottom teeth, but this time do not push as hard as you did for the "eeee" or the buzz tone.
2. Make an extended "a" sound as in the word "cat." Try to elongate this lower sound up to 20 seconds over a period of time.
3. If you are making this sound correctly, you should feel a vibrating sensation in your throat.

In everyday speech you use two breath streams, the upper and the lower (see Illus. 4). The upper breath stream is for vibrating sounds like mmm, ng, er and z.

The lower breath stream is for vowels as in "hay" and "slay." If you plug your nose, you will notice that you can say the hay, slay sounds. The tongue, if placed firmly behind the bottom teeth as already described, will direct more of the air through the nasal passages. Note that you only place your tongue here to cause the upper and lower breath streams to divide correctly. When the dummy is speaking, the tip of your tongue is moving inside the mouth. *If you feel your nose, you will find it vibrates a bit if you are making the dummy voice correctly.*

Since there are two breath streams, the dummy's voice is more diffuse and this makes it hard to locate.

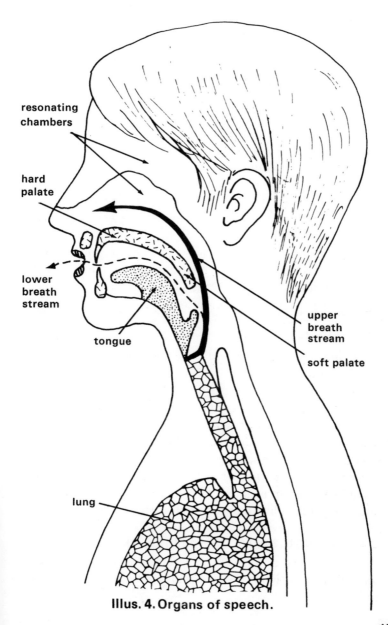

resonating
chambers

hard
palate

lower
breath
stream

tongue

upper
breath
stream

soft palate

lung

Illus. 4. Organs of speech.

To make the dummy voice with double divided breath streams: Take a deep breath and extend the sound of "ng" as in "sing" and then add a word containing a vowel sound like "kay." Elongate the sound and it will look like this: nnnnnnnnnnnnnnnngggggggggggggggg-kaaaaaaaaaaaay.

When you pinch your nose, you should hear the lower breath stream vowel sounds of "kay." When you cover your mouth you should hear the resonating sounds of "nnnnnnnnng-nnnnnnnnnnnnng" coming from the nose. Finally, extending the word "slaaaaaaaaay" will help you to find the right tone for the dummy's voice. You should then say daily the beginner's alphabet and the vowels i, e, a, o, u, in the "slay" tone.

The ventriloquist voice is not made by a grunt but the flow of air is controlled by contracting the muscles of the diaphragm just above the waist. If you are making the voice correctly, your nose will vibrate slightly.

Hard sounds made easy

You have already seen with the beginner's alphabet that there are certain letters which cannot be said without moving the lips. The letters "b" and "p" are called "explosives" because in forming them a slight popping sound is made with the lips. The letters "v" and "f" are only partly explosive. To say these letters, you press your lower lip lightly against the upper teeth. When saying the letter "m," you press your lips lightly together.

So the ventriloquist must find a new way to make these sounds—or find substitutes for them—without moving lips.

Sound substitutes for B (see Illus. 4)

Your tongue starts behind your bottom teeth, below them, and as the sound is made the tip of your tongue rises to the hard palate.

The substitute sound you use will depend on the shape of your mouth inside.

Sound of B: think "b" but say "d."

Sound of B: think "b" but say "t."

Here is the one that I use.

Sound of B: think "b" but say "vh" (letting a little air out at the same time).

Try all the substitutes for B and then pick the one that sounds the best to you. "I'd like a nice cold bottle of beer" with substitutions becomes: "I'd like a nice cold vh-ottle of vh-eer." It is important that you put more *stress* on the *last* part of the word vh-ottle. Practice with these for the letter B.

Go down below. What about the old banjo?

Go down vh-low. What about the old vhanjo?

Practice these in front of a mirror for about (avhout) half an hour and you will notice an improvement.

Sound substitute for F

Sound of F: think "f" but say "th."

Sound of F: think "f" but put an "h" sound in front of the word.

"Father" becomes "thather."

"Father" becomes "hather."

The -ather part of "father" should be said a little *louder*. Practice these:

(a) I run very fast.

(b) Father finds candy for fun.

(c) Finish your fudge bar (vhar) now.

Sound substitute for V

Put your tongue behind your bottom teeth at first.

Sound of V: think "v" but say "th."

Sound of V: think "v" but try and say a soft "v" sound

and make your voice a litle higher on the last syllable of the word.

Practice these sentences:

(a) I go very fast (th-ery fast).

(b) I think that is *very* funny.

(c) Veal, vain, Valerie, Vince.

Sound substitute for M (see Illus. 4)

Place your tongue well below the bottom teeth as in Illus. 3 on page 17, but a little lower.

1. Make an "ng" sound with a slight humming before it.
2. As you say the word "Mary" your tongue goes from below your bottom teeth to the roof of your mouth or the hard palate (see page 19).

   "Mary had a little lamb" with substitutes becomes:

   "ng-ary had a little la-ng-uh."

   Keep saying the humming sound in front of the -ng and the last syllables of Mary (ary). Say it slowly like a child trying to sound a new word, and then try to run it all together.
3. It is important that you should put a little more stress on the part of the word -ary.

   Practice this sentence:

   Mary wants to bring a very fine pencil.

Sound substitute for P (see Illus. 4)

Put your tongue below and behind the bottom teeth and as you say the sound substitute for "p" the tip of your tongue goes to the roof of your mouth.

Sound of P: think "p" but say "t."

Sound of P: think "p" but say "k."

Sound of P: think "p" but say the last syllable with more stress.

Practice until you find the substitute that suits you best.

Listen to your substitutes on a tape recorder as a way of picking the best one.

The substitutes become more effective if you expel a little air from the mouth as you are saying them. Practice these words in front of a mirror:

Please, polish, practice, prairie, pride, prison, privilege, porridge.

Sound substitute for W

When you are saying the alphabet, say "duvhle-u." When you are saying the "w" sound in a word, make the "w" into two syllables.

Think "w" but say "ooooooooo-ant" for "want."

Say oooooo-ant, oooant slowly. Now speed up a bit, putting the two sounds together and it will soon sound like "want." Practice the following sentences:

(a) Wee Willy Wilson wanted Walter Watson's watch.

(b) I want to go very fast, Freddy.

(c) I don't think that's very funny, Willy.

Try these words in front of a mirror. Funny, fussy, fairy, fast, Fred, for, finish, forest.

Now go back and practice all the sentences and words.

The muffled voice

When you have perfected the near ventriloquial voice, you can try this one, which creates the illusion that the dummy is speaking from a cupboard or closed suitcase. The voice is still very strong but is lacking in clarity. Follow these step-by-step instructions, have confidence in yourself and your partner, and you will be surprised at the impact you can have with this trick.

1. Take a full breath.
2. Arch your tongue back as in Illus. 5. This will cause your voice to have a muffled effect as though you were speaking

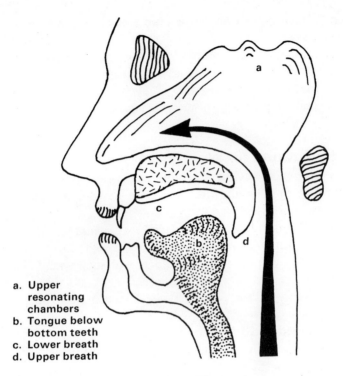

a. Upper
   resonating
   chambers
b. Tongue below
   bottom teeth
c. Lower breath
d. Upper breath

Illus. 5. Muffled voice.

with a mouthful of marbles. This arching or curling of the tongue tends to close or constrict the throat and the voice is channeled back and up into the nasal passages.

Muffled voice

3. This voice is made farther back in the throat, unlike the near ventriloquial voice which is brought up into the front of the mouth as much as possible.

4. Put your hand a little above your waist line. Say a long . . . sssssssssssssssss . . . sound as loudly as you can. Can you feel your diaphragm muscles pushing this "ssss" sound out under pressure?
5. When you do the muffled voice you must use the same muscles as when making the "ssss" sound explained in point 4. This puts the voice under pressure as though it were trying to escape from the suitcase.

Acting out the part will help to heighten the illusion that the voice is actually coming from the suitcase.

If you want to use the muffled voice to close your act, you must get the dummy into the suitcase convincingly, with his voice becoming fainter as the lid closes. Let the audience see your lips. Don't hide behind the suitcase lid. Here is a routine you could work on:
1. Put your hand up to your ear and say "I thought that I heard something."
2. Bend your knees and get a little closer to the case.
3. Say "What was that? . . . You want to get out!" Since the voice is lacking in clarity, I feel that it is a good idea to tell the audience what your partner is going to say before he says it or after he has said it.

I use the same phrase every time so that I can create the illusion that the voice is getting more muffled as the lid is closing. This can be achieved by following these steps:
1. When the lid is open do the near-ventriloquial voice at a louder level.
2. When the lid is completely closed, curl the tongue as in Illus. 5; this causes the voice to have much less clarity.
"Let me out of here" now sounds like
"et ee ow o ere."

Notice that the initial consonants are lost because of the lack of clarity.

The distant voice

The distant voice is another effective trick but as it is very faint, it does not have the same entertainment possibilities as the muffled and the near-ventriloquial voices.

Steps in making the distant voice

1. Make the "drone" as explained on page 18.
2. Arch the tongue as in Illus. 3 on page 17, until the throat is almost closed.
3. Prolong the aaaaaaaaaahhhhhhhhhh "drone" sound one octave higher.
4. At the same time push upward with your diaphragm muscles to direct the sound to the uppermost part of your resonating chambers (see page 20).
5. Try to produce a steady tone. Do not practice for long periods at a time.

Finally try to say words and short phrases in this high "droning" tone.

STANLEY: I can throw my voice down to the cellar.
VENTRILOQUIST: I don't think that you can do it!
STANLEY: Oh, yes I can!
VENTRILOQUIST: O.K. Let me hear you. (I think that this is his first time so don't be too hard on him).
STANLEY: *(Bends over and looks towards the floor.)*
  HELLO . . . DOWN THERE!
Voice from cellar: Hello, how are you?
STANLEY: I'm fine, thanks. What are you doing down there?
Voice from cellar: I'm shoveling coal.
STANLEY: When are you coming up?
  (............ *long pause* .... *no answer* ....)
VENTRILOQUIST: Why is there no answer?
STANLEY: He must have shut the cellar door!

When presenting the distant voice to an audience it has more impact if the whole routine is carefully acted out.

So much for the techniques. But your partner must become a definite personality with a consistent voice in contrast with your own. Listen to young children and copy their interesting inflections and expressions; this can also help you with the voice contrast. Below I have listed a few ways in which you can obtain a good contrast.

(a) When you are speaking, exaggerate your lip movements and the clarity of your speech.

(b) The dummy's voice must be higher or lower than your own voice.

(c) You could make the dummy speak faster or slower than yourself.

(d) He might even make some grammatical mistakes as well.

(e) The dummy could have either a regional or a foreign accent.

(f) Put your routines on a tape recorder to enable you to test for a good contrast and distant voice effects.

Remember, a good contrast in the dummy's voice will help to reinforce its lifelike qualities.

4. Manipulating the Dummy

You can now make your dummy speak with an individual voice, and you can do it without moving your lips. But so far the dummy itself is just a block of wood or other inert material. You now come to the point of making him into a person with a unique character of his own.

First of all, it is most important to analyze your own character carefully so that when you create the dummy's character there is a good contrast. According to Freud, all of us have hidden desires that we suppress. The most successful ventriloquists have let these hidden desires be expressed in the personality of their dummies.

The manner in which your dummy is manipulated or moved should be tailored to suit its character. Mortimer Snerd, an unintelligent country bumpkin, moves his head slowly and quite often his mouth is partially open after he has finished speaking.

Before you can create a character you should become a "people watcher." This means that you should watch people while they are angry, surprised, happy and shy in order to observe the body language that goes with these expressions. A surprised person, for example, might be wide-eyed and open-mouthed. Try to copy the head and eye movements in front of a full-length mirror. The chart is intended only as a framework upon which I am certain my fellow ventriloquists will elaborate.

Expression	How to manipulate the dummy
Flirting	wink one eye, raise eyebrow
Laughing	move headstick back and forth in jerks
Surprise	mouth open, body moves back a bit
Deep thought	head up, eyes partly closed, still
Ashamed	head lowered, looks out of corners of eyes
Stupidity	slow movements, mouth partially open
Eagerness	forward movements of body
Slyness	head in body, eyes partially closed
Crying	same as laughing, rest head on shoulders
Complaining	whining tone of voice, shaking head

The following general principles of figure manipulation will help you to create a more lifelike illusion.

1. Never make quick, mechanical movements. They should appear natural and lifelike.
2. When operating the mouth lever always pull it ONCE for EACH SYLLABLE.

   Hel/lo/how/are/you/? (5 movements of lever required)

   Hey/you've/got/the/wrong/guy/in/the/suit/case! (10 movements needed)

   I/don't/want/the/op/er/a/tion (8 movements of the lever required)

   This/is/the/on/ly/way/to/do/the/job. (10 movements are needed here)

   It is possible to practice mouth movements when your partner isn't with you by constructing a practice mouth control lever from an old broomstick. A heavy elastic or spring attached to the side of the dowel would give the correct tension to the lever. This device will strengthen the muscles of your thumb. (See Illus. 6 on page 30).
3. Look at your figure when he is speaking to you and if he tells you off, look angry. When he tells a funny joke, laugh at it.

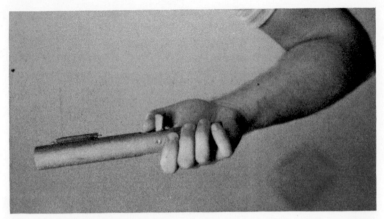

Illus. 6. Practice stick—a mouth control lever stick enables the ventriloquist to practice mouth movements without using a dummy.

4. Move the head forward slightly to stress certain words (No, I won't!).
5. Some ventriloquists like to turn the dummy's head completely around in the socket in order to get a laugh. In my opinion this stunt destroys the illusion of life and is not a good idea.

General instructions for manipulation

Look at Illus. 7. The right hand is usually curled around the headstick (c) with the thumb on the front lever (f) which controls the mouth movements. The first and second fingers are on the back levers labeled (d). These levers usually operate side eye movements, closing of the eyelids and the raising of the eyebrows.

You can buy animated figures that can walk mechanically, smoke, cry, spit, stick out their tongues and light up their nose and wiggle their ears when a good-looking girl comes along.

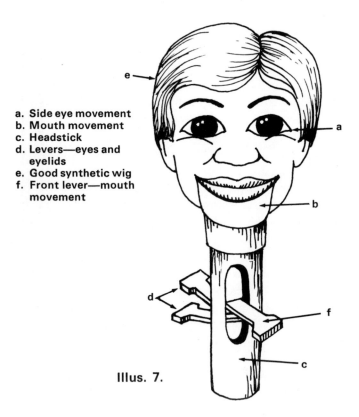

a. Side eye movement
b. Mouth movement
c. Headstick
d. Levers—eyes and eyelids
e. Good synthetic wig
f. Front lever—mouth movement

Illus. 7.

These features are expensive and make the dummy look mechanical.

It is possible to move the head of the figure sideways or in a nodding fashion by a mere movement of the wrist. Remember to make your movements smooth and lifelike.

Since manufacturers use many different ways to animate figures, you must experiment with your own in order to discover the best possible way to manipulate it. The best figures have movements operated by wooden or metal levers. Cheaper ones have strings with rings attached, but these are more difficult to operate. Manipulation can best be practiced by acting out an imaginary situation in pantomime (movement only; no sound). Imagine that a beautiful girl walks past you and your partner and drops her handkerchief. She then begins to play Ping-Pong with a friend. The ball rolls off the table and onto the floor. Your partner now thinks that this is very amusing and starts to laugh.

This pantomime should be practiced in front of a full-length mirror so that every expression and movement can be perfected.

More audience impact is obtained during a ventriloquist act if your partner comes to life and is endowed with a "certain separateness." Ventriloquists who achieve public acclaim are normally master manipulators of their dummies and endow them with a personality that is separate from their own. In the following paragraphs I shall attempt to show ventriloquists how they can achieve this magical quality of "separateness."

Inanimate objects come to life in a magician's hands through manipulative skill and hidden gimmicks. The magician at times seems to have very little control over the objects which in reality he operates. An example here would be the Zombie Floating Ball Effect where the ball has apparently gained enough power to pull the performer around the stage. At times the cloth seems to escape from the magician's hands which tends to reinforce the lifelike qualities of the object.

As we shall see in Chapter 7, an important comparison exists in figure manipulation in ventriloquism. Most beginners in ventriloquism expend all their energy controlling lip movement and the lip movement of their partner and as a result of this they have very little time left to create a deceptive illusion in which their figure is a "separate" personality.

Some amateur acts consist of a ventriloquist feeding a line to the dummy and the dummy replying, with very little happening in between. You should react to your little partner. When he says something funny, laugh and when he insults you, look upset and angry.

Timing, although difficult to attain, is of the utmost importance. When your partner insults you, you should simultaneously look angry and shake your head back and forth. Constant practice in front of a full-length mirror will help you to achieve this illusion.

Here is another situation which gives the audience the impression that your dummy has a personality of its own with the ability to continue an action while the ventriloquist is talking. Make your figure cough to clear his throat before he sings a song. Start him coughing loudly and gradually make him get quieter. Ask him "Are you ready to sing?" While you are asking him the question, he should continue with the short jerky forward movements, his mouth partially open. This movement of the dummy simulates the coughing action. As soon as you have finished asking the question, faint coughing sounds are heard again. Some people will actually believe that your partner coughed while you were talking.

It is possible for you and your figure to talk simultaneously with mechanical contrivances such as tape recorders. This illusion can partially be achieved by making your partner simulate the action of coughing, crying or laughing while you are talking.

To create a deceptive illusion you should always practice in front of a full-length mirror so that you can react to your figure with the appropriate facial expression. Believe in the illusion that you are creating.

5. Planning Your Routine

ROUTINES can vary in length from 1 to 15 minutes; for the beginner, I would suggest a routine lasting 1 or 2 minutes. If a routine is more than 5 minutes long it should have cut-off points so that it can be shortened if the audience is noisy or unreceptive.

Joke books, magazines and newspapers are good sources of material for dialogues, as are comedy scripts used on radio and television programs. Make a list of all the jokes you feel are potential laugh-getters, arrange them according to subject (girls, farm animals, money, etc.).

Quiz shows
VENTRILOQUIST: Where is the capital of America?
STANLEY: All over Europe!

VENTRILOQUIST: What would you do if your brakes suddenly stopped working?
STANLEY: I'd guess I'd try to hit something cheap.

Girls
VENTRILOQUIST: When did you first like girls?
STANLEY: When I discovered that they *weren't boys*!

When you are planning a routine don't merely write down a series of unrelated jokes; think of a theme or story and then select jokes that follow each other along this theme. An example could be "Troubles with the Girl Friend."

The following summary of general principles will help you to plan a routine that will elicit a good audience reaction.

Ways of organizing a dialogue

(a) Memorize it perfectly so that you can concentrate on the audience reaction.

(b) Put your second-best joke near the beginning of the routine. The last joke should be the best of your routine.

(c) To make the routine sound natural, try to blend every joke into each other. Here is an example that demonstrates changing from one subject to another within a routine.

VENTRILOQUIST: I thought that you were a gentleman!

STANLEY: What's a gentleman?

VENTRILOQUIST: Well, when a young lady comes into a room, what do you do?

STANLEY: Whistle!

VENTRILOQUIST: No! When a young lady comes into a room, you tip your hat and bow. What does that show?

STANLEY: The hole in my trousers!

VENTRILOQUIST: If you are old enough to be interested in girls, you are certainly old enough to go to school! Do you go to school?

STANLEY: Of course . . . when I can't get out of it!

When writing a routine, imagine that you are a reporter interviewing kids about their trip to the farm, for example. You might call the dialogue "Farmyard Frolics." Some possible questions might be: "Why did you decide to visit a farm? How long did you decide to stay? What animal did you take a fancy to? Do you like to do chores?"

Another technique used in writing dialogues is to take a well known story or poem and make your partner continually interrupt your story at several places in the plot. Here is the start of a routine called "'Twas the Night before Christmas."

VENTRILOQUIST: Well, Stanley, Christmas time is here again. Have you made out your Christmas list yet?

35

STANLEY: Of course I have.

VENTRILOQUIST: What have you put on your list?

STANLEY: A new Cadillac, a stereo record player, a dishwasher, and a color television.

VENTRILOQUIST: Are you giving expensive gifts like that?

STANLEY: Giving! Giving! No! That's what I want to get!

VENTRILOQUIST: You should be ashamed of yourself. You know it's more blessed to give than to receive.

STANLEY: What was that?

VENTRILOQUIST: I said it is more blessed to give than to receive.

STANLEY: Ah! Bless you. I'll take all you want to give.

VENTRILOQUIST: When Santa Claus comes down your chimney on Christmas Eve what would you like to find in your stocking?

STANLEY: *(short silence while he looks around the room)* That good-looking girl in the front row!

VENTRILOQUIST: Oh! For goodness sake!

STANLEY: Oh no, *for fun! for fun!*

VENTRILOQUIST: And now ladies and gentlemen I am going to tell a Christmas story.

(Stanley tries to get away but you pull him back by the arm.)

STANLEY: Ohhhhhhhhhhhh! Here I go.

VENTRILOQUIST: Stanley, do you know "'Twas the Night before Christmas"?

STANLEY: *Already?*

VENTRILOQUIST: "'Twas the night before Christmas and all through the house . . ."

STANLEY: It was cold and dreary as the furnace went out.

VENTRILOQUIST: Oh stop interrupting! "Not a creature was stirring, not even a . . ."

STANLEY: *(butts in)* Not even a cockroach?

VENTRILOQUIST: "The stockings were hung by the chimney with care, In hopes . . ."

STANLEY: In hopes that your wife wouldn't find them in the morning. *(This might only be suitable for an all adult audience.)*

On the other hand for children situation comedy has more impact than jokes. For example the same line could be:

STANLEY: In hopes that they would be dry by morning.

This line is not funny in itself but the idea of the dummy ruining the story with inane comments is sufficient to evoke laughter.

The Quiz Show format

In using the quiz show format, you should play the part of the quiz master questioning your partner, using a series of jokes and riddles revolving around famous persons, places or things. Here is a sample of the type of material that you could use:

VENTRILOQUIST: I would like to give you a test to show the children how intelligent you are.
STANLEY: Can't they tell just by looking at me?
VENTRILOQUIST: No, they can't. Now in what direction does the Hudson River flow?
STANLEY: DOWNHILL!
VENTRILOQUIST: Where was the Queen crowned?
STANLEY: On her head, of course!
VENTRILOQUIST: Where was the Declaration of Independence signed?
STANLEY: AT THE BOTTOM!
VENTRILOQUIST: Why is a politician like a puppeteer?
STANLEY: He's always pulling strings!
VENTRILOQUIST: I'm not laughing!
STANLEY: If I had a face like yours, I wouldn't laugh either.

Children particularly like this type of routine as your partner always gets the answers wrong.

"A producer can purchase applause with money or passes, but he cannot purchase laughter. Laughing is something that an audience takes pleasure in paying to do." *(Ashton Stevens)*

Laughter is a very important ingredient of modern ventriloquism and ventriloquism without laughter is like apple pie without cheese. How does one create laughter among the audience? First of all, every ventriloquist should study the psychology of laughter to gain a better understanding of the mechanisms that cause an audience to laugh out loud. Psychologists experimenting with young babies have discovered that the greatest degree of laughter was obtained when the psychologist swung the babies towards their mother's arms, but just before they arrived, they were pulled back quickly. Basically, laughter occurs by guiding the minds of the audience towards an anticipated goal, then just before arriving, playfully misdirecting them to a different conclusion. Having a good understanding of why people laugh will equip the ventriloquist or comedian to construct dialogues which will be amusing. When working out dialogue routines you should avoid political, religious and ethnic types of material and *never* use off-color material. If you do not agree with this advice, then you should be sure that you know your audience well and that these routines are acceptable to it.

Since early impressions of the audience tend to suggest how laugh-provoking the rest of your routine will be, it is important to have a funny opening for your dialogue. Here are two examples of opening lines that you might like to use in your routine:

VENTRILOQUIST: What a wonderful-looking audience. Look at all of those smiling faces out there.

STANLEY: What else could they do but *smile* when *you* walked out!

or

VENTRILOQUIST: Well, funny face, what would you like to do to entertain this wonderful audience?

STANLEY: You should talk! Have you ever looked in a mirror?

VENTRILOQUIST: Quite often, my boy!

STANLEY: And frightened himself half to death every time!

At my Christmas performances Stanley sings "Deck the Hall" as we walk off the stage and as he hits the last note it is twice as loud and very sour. As it is an unexpected surprise, it results in laughter.

Another example would be:

VENTRILOQUIST: Can I help you, Stanley?

STANLEY: I lost my chewing gum *(moves head forward and from side to side as if searching for something).*

VENTRILOQUIST: Oh, I thought it was important!

STANLEY: *It was! My teeth were in it.*

The repetition of certain words or movements by your partner will help to create laughter among the audience. One example would be if you were performing informally and a beautiful girl walked by. Have your partner raise his eyebrows several times. Another example would be if you wanted your partner to sing a song and he refuses by bellowing, "No! I won't sing."

Have him do this several times and then grab him by the lapel. Stanley then says in an angry tone, "Get your cotton-pickin' hands off the suit!"

Below is another example of some repetitive dialogue:

VENTRILOQUIST: I have a girl friend something like her.

STANLEY: Olé!

VENTRILOQUIST: Come to think of it, I have about 10 girls like her.

STANLEY: Olé!

VENTRILOQUIST: Why do you keep saying Olé?

STANLEY: Well that's what they say when you bring out the *bull*!

Stanley's opinion of me is not very high at times. He believes me to be penurious because of his own allowance of 50¢ per week. He makes jokes about my weight and about my importance in front of other people. He even plays practical jokes on me like the black-eye gag explained in another part of the book. The audience expects Stanley to deflate people, play boyish pranks, get into scrapes and out again as boys will.

In the routine called "She Doesn't Love Me Anymore" (see page 48) Stanley is portrayed as a real swinger as he reluctantly reveals his playboy techniques. After he has turned off the lights, closed the curtains, turned the music down low and sat down very close on the sofa, it turns out that all that has occurred is that he has been watching a Western on the television. The suspense created gives more impact to the surprise ending.

Laughter is obtained in situation comedy not by the jokes, but by the amusing predicament created. Good acting and timing is important in creating a good situation comedy.

VENTRILOQUIST: What were you and Charlie doing, Stanley?

STANLEY: We were practicing our Boy Scout life-saving routine when along came Skinny Morgan and obligingly jumped into the water with his clothes on.

VENTRILOQUIST: That doesn't sound like Skinny.

STANLEY: Well, . . . No *(in a sheepish tone of voice)* . . . *(long pause)* . . . well, he sort of had a dizzy spell, too.

VENTRILOQUIST: He had a dizzy spell and jumped in.

STANLEY: . . . err, ah, not exactly. He kind . . . of slipped, . . . too.

VENTRILOQUIST: He had a dizzy spell, he slipped? He had a dizzy spell, he slipped . . .

STANLEY: *(in a loud angry voice) All right, I pushed him in!*

Some ventriloquists like to hypnotize their partners. First, they have them sway back and forth, as their eyelids become heavy and slowly close.

VENTRILOQUIST: Notice, ladies and gentlemen, Stanley is completely asleep. *(As you are saying this, Stanley opens one eye slowly and giggles a bit to himself.)*

Wait for the audience to laugh first and then look towards Stanley quickly. Of course Stanley is much too quick for me and manages to close his eye before I notice it. Proper pausing and lifelike manipulation will create a shower of laughter among the audience.

 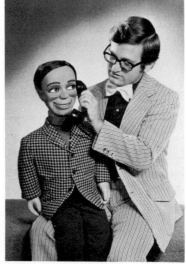

Illus. 8. The telephone conversation is another good basis for a dialogue routine, especially when you pass the phone to your partner, who makes the whole situation very amusing.

Sometimes by telling the truth in a *natural* way, it becomes hilarious. Edgar Bergen's Mortimer Snerd, a country bumpkin in personality and dress, sometimes says: "You'd never think I was raised on a farm, would you?"

Here are some lines suitable for this rustic type of personality:

VENTRILOQUIST: What makes you so stupid?
STANLEY: Well, I just let nature take its course!

or

VENTRILOQUIST: Why are you so unintelligent?
STANLEY: I don't know, but whatever it is *it works!*

Laughter will be created by stretching or exaggerating the truth. Here are some sample dialogue lines:

STANLEY: The doctor made me take three bottles of pills.
VENTRILOQUIST: What's so hard about taking three bottles of pills?
STANLEY: The bottles kept getting stuck in my throat!

or

STANLEY: My cow gives 600 quarts of milk a day!
VENTRILOQUIST: That's a lot of milk!
STANLEY: *That's a lot of bull, too!*

Keep in mind the age and the degree of sophistication of your audience when using humor involving puns or a play on words.

VENTRILOQUIST: This is the second time that your teacher has caught you with your homework not completed. It's about time that you should learn to *rely* upon yourself!
STANLEY: *Don't worry about me,* I can *lie* with the *best* of them!

After Stanley has successfully spelled the word defeat he is asked to use it in a sentence.

STANLEY: Tight shoes hurt dee feet.

VENTRILOQUIST: Did you like this speech, Stanley?
STANLEY: I think it looks like a steer.
VENTRILOQUIST: What do you mean, it looks like a steer?
STANLEY: Well you made a point here and a point there and had a lot of bull in between!

VENTRILOQUIST: How would you like to be the judge of a dog show? But just a minute, you don't know anything about dogs.
STANLEY: Oh yeah, you should have seen the girl that I was out with last night . . . a real dog!
VENTRILOQUIST: I don't believe you.
STANLEY: Just a minute I'll bring the one in that I left tied to the fire hydrant.

VENTRILOQUIST: Please spell the word "new."
STANLEY: N . . . E . . . W . . .
VENTRILOQUIST: Very good. Now spell the word canoe.
STANLEY: K . . . N . . . E . . . W.

STANLEY: You remind me of the vast ocean.
VENTRILOQUIST: Romantic, turbulent, and restless?
STANLEY: No, you just make me s-i-c-k!

Laughter is all a matter of perspective. Meeting a girl in a revolving door is not that funny, but when Stanley complains that he has been going round and round with her ever since, it creates a few chuckles in the audience.

If you study professional ventriloquists' and comedians' routines from radio or TV, you will discover that they use contemporary humor and an ever varying array of techniques to make an audience laugh.

6. Professional Dialogues

Miscellaneous madness (warm-up patter)

STANLEY: What makes a balloon go up into the air?

VENTRILOQUIST: Well, you know a balloon is a big bag of gas or hot air. Naturally anything filled with hot air rises.

STANLEY: Well then, WHAT'S HOLDING YOU DOWN?

STANLEY: Did your father ever lift weights?

VENTRILOQUIST: No, why?

STANLEY: Well, how in the heck did he raise a dumbbell like you?

STANLEY: You remind me of Whistler's Mother standing up.

VENTRILOQUIST: Why do you say that?

STANLEY: You're off your rocker!

STANLEY: I'm looking for a song that goes igga-aka-hicky, icky-wacha-ding-a-ring-a-ling.

VENTRILOQUIST: What are the words for the song?

STANLEY: Those are the words, ding-a-ling.

STANLEY: I'm going to buy me a farm 2 miles long and $\frac{1}{4}$ inch wide.

VENTRILOQUIST: What on earth could you raise on a farm that size?

STANLEY: Spaghetti!

VENTRILOQUIST: What did the doctor say about your heavy smoking?

STANLEY: He said that I should change my habits.

VENTRILOQUIST: Did you change?

STANLEY: I sure did! I changed doctors too!

STANLEY: Doc, every time I drink a cup of tea, I get a sharp pain in my eye. What do you think I should do?

VENTRILOQUIST: Take the spoon out of your cup.

STANLEY: I didn't sleep too well last night.
VENTRILOQUIST: What was the matter?
STANLEY: I plugged my electric blanket in the toaster and kept POPPING out of bed all night.

VENTRILOQUIST: What did you do, Stanley, when the boat sank in the middle of the ocean?
STANLEY: I grabbed a cake of Lifebuoy and washed myself ashore.

VENTRILOQUIST: Name two pronouns.
STANLEY: Who, me?
VENTRILOQUIST: That's absolutely right.

VENTRILOQUIST: How would you like a job as a singing bird caller?
STANLEY: Wonderful, Tweet, tweet, YUCK!
                            Tweet, tweet, YUCK!
VENTRILOQUIST: What's the YUCK for?
STANLEY: Have you ever eaten a worm, man?

VENTRILOQUIST: How many sexes are there?
STANLEY: There are three.
VENTRILOQUIST: What! . . . Well, what are they?
STANLEY: The female sex, the male sex and the in-sex (insects!).

(at end of a routine)
VENTRILOQUIST: Au revoir!
STANLEY: What does that mean?
VENTRILOQUIST: That's good-bye in French.
STANLEY: ARSENIC!
VENTRILOQUIST: What's that?
STANLEY: THAT'S GOOD-BYE IN ANY LANGUAGE!

Report Card Time is Here Again

Stanley sneezes several times and says:

STANLEY: I've got seen-us trouble.

VENTRILOQUIST: You mean sinus trouble, don't you?

STANLEY: No!, Seen-us trouble. You see, we were cheating on the exams, the teacher walked in and *seen us and were we in trouble!*

VENTRILOQUIST: What is that in your pocket?

STANLEY: Nothing.

VENTRILOQUIST: I can see something yellow in your pocket.

STANLEY: *(interrupting very quickly)* Can you sign your name with your eyes closed?

VENTRILOQUIST: I suppose so. Why do you ask?

STANLEY: Well, would you mind closing your eyes to sign my report card?

VENTRILOQUIST: No! I want to see your report card right now.

STANLEY: *(sighs)* Oh no!

VENTRILOQUIST: What kind of marks did you get this term?

STANLEY: Well, they are all under water.

VENTRILOQUIST: I don't understand. What do you mean?

STANLEY: They're all *below sea level.*

VENTRILOQUIST: *(takes report card from dummy's pocket)* Let me see now. Geography 47%, History 48%, *Mathematics!* Why is your mark in Mathematics so low?

STANLEY: It's all your fault!

VENTRILOQUIST: My fault? I don't understand.

STANLEY: If it wasn't for your magic card tricks I wouldn't have failed my first exam.

VENTRILOQUIST: What do you mean?

STANLEY: Well, the teacher asked me to count from 1 to 20.

VENTRILOQUIST: What did you do?

STANLEY: I . . . ah . . . said 1 . . . 2 . . . 3 . . . 4 . . . 5 . . . 6 . . . 7 . . . 8 . . . 9 . . . 10 . . . *jack . . . queen . . . king!*

VENTRILOQUIST: You are a real blockhead!

STANLEY: I was carved that way. What's your excuse?

VENTRILOQUIST: Stop all this nonsense! I want to show these boys and girls that you are very intelligent.

STANLEY: Can't they tell by looking?

VENTRILOQUIST: No, they can't. Now here's a problem for you. Have you got a quarter?

STANLEY: I haven't got a quarter.

VENTRILOQUIST: Use your imagination!

STANLEY: I haven't got that much imagination!

VENTRILOQUIST: Now listen. Pretend that you have a quarter and then you give me a dime. How much would you have left?

STANLEY: Ahhhh . . . ahhhh . . . a quarter.

VENTRILOQUIST: You don't get my meaning!

STANLEY: *And you don't get my quarter!*

VENTRILOQUIST: Can you spell the word defeat?

STANLEY: D . . . ah . . . E . . . What comes next?

VENTRILOQUIST: F is next.

STANLEY: D . . . E . . . F . . . What comes next?

VENTRILOQUIST: E is next. Would you like me to spell the whole word?

STANLEY: We'd do better if you would.

VENTRILOQUIST: Stop messing about and spell the word "defeat."

STANLEY: D . . . E . . . F . . . E . . . A . . . T

VENTRILOQUIST: Amazing! Give me a sentence using the word "defeat."

STANLEY: All right. Twenty years in jail!

VENTRILOQUIST: No, give me a sentence using the word defeat.

STANLEY: Ah . . . ah . . . Tight shoes hurt dee feet!

VENTRILOQUIST: Do you know school days?

STANLEY: Yes, I'd love no school days.

VENTRILOQUIST: I mean do you know the song "School Days"?

Finish the routine with the song "School Days." Alternate the lines of the song and give yourself the lines with the most difficult substitutions in them.

SCHOOL DAYS
School days, school days,
Dear old golden rule days,
Reading, writing, and arithmetic,
Taught to the tune of a hickory stick.
I was your queen in calico,
You were my bashful, barefoot beau.
I wrote on your slate,
I love you, Kate
When we were a couple of kids.

She Doesn't Love Me Any More

VENTRILOQUIST: It certainly is a pleasure to see all those smiling faces out there.

STANLEY: What else could you do but *smile* when he walked out.

VENTRILOQUIST: This certainly is a lovely audience.

STANLEY: Yes, my girl friend is sitting out there.

VENTRILOQUIST: What does she look like?

STANLEY: You see the girl in the first row with the blond hair?

VENTRILOQUIST: Yes.

STANLEY: The gorgeous brown eyes and the good-looking figure?

VENTRILOQUIST: Yes! Is that your girl friend?

STANLEY: No! She's the *ugly one* sitting next to her!

VENTRILOQUIST: I heard that you met your girl friend in a revolving door.

STANLEY: Yes, and I've been going round and round with her ever since *(moving his head in a circular fashion)*.

VENTRILOQUIST: Now, Stanley, you've been engaged for several years. Why have you never bothered to marry?

STANLEY: You know getting married is like falling in a sewer.

VENTRILOQUIST: What in the world has getting married got to do with falling in a sewer?

STANLEY: Either way you look at it, it's sewer-side!

VENTRILOQUIST: You're just biased when it comes to women.

STANLEY: That's why I haven't got any money! It's always bias this, bias that.

VENTRILOQUIST: I've heard that you're a real swinger at weekends.

STANLEY: Yes, I take her to a rather sexy little hotel in the country.

VENTRILOQUIST: What goes on there?

STANLEY: Well, first I *lock* the door.

VENTRILOQUIST: And then . . .

STANLEY: I close the curtains.

VENTRILOQUIST: And then what happens?

STANLEY: I turn off all the lights.

VENTRILOQUIST: Very interesting!

STANLEY: Turn down the bed covers.

VENTRILOQUIST: *(excited)* Then what happens next?

STANLEY: I turn on the television and we watch Westerns.

VENTRILOQUIST: Watch Westerns? Is that all you ever do?

STANLEY: We've seen so many Westerns that we've got saddlebags under our eyes!

VENTRILOQUIST: You are next to an idiot!

STANLEY: Then why don't you move?

VENTRILOQUIST: Is that all you ever do, chase girls?

STANLEY: No, sometimes I catch them!

VENTRILOQUIST: What happens if your girl friend finds out?

STANLEY: Well, if she finds out, I *get out* before she starts to strangle me!

VENTRILOQUIST: I thought you were a black belt?

STANLEY: Yeah, but she had a brown one.

VENTRILOQUIST: I thought that a black belt was superior to a brown one?

STANLEY: Yes, but her belt was *around my neck.*

VENTRILOQUIST: Oh! You had a fight with your girl friend?

STANLEY: *(hangs his head, ashamed)* Yes.

VENTRILOQUIST: Tell me what she did. I want to get to the bottom of things.

STANLEY: First, she hit me on the face.

VENTRILOQUIST: And then?

STANLEY: She shook me by the shoulders.

VENTRILOQUIST: Go on!

STANLEY: She pulled my hair!

VENTRILOQUIST: Yes!

STANLEY: She kicked me!

VENTRILOQUIST: Where did she kick you?

STANLEY: Now you're at the *bottom of things!*

VENTRILOQUIST: She sounds like a real live wire.

STANLEY: Yes, you should see her insulation—boy!

VENTRILOQUIST: Have you got any other hobbies besides girls?

STANLEY: I like to hunt.

VENTRILOQUIST: What kind of game do you hunt?

STANLEY: Blonds, brunettes and redheads!

VENTRILOQUIST: You spend so much time talking and thinking about girls. Don't you realize that there are more important things? After all women are a dime a dozen.

STANLEY: What was that you just said?

VENTRILOQUIST: I said, women are a dime a dozen.

STANLEY: And all this time I've been wasting my money on jelly beans.

VENTRILOQUIST: Imagine that you have your girl friend out for the evening. The air is scented, the crickets are chirping, the moon is out . . .

STANLEY: And so are her parents!

VENTRILOQUIST: What would you do out there?

STANLEY: I'd recite a little verse for her.

VENTRILOQUIST: Let's hear it.

STANLEY: Twinkle, twinkle, little star,
How I wonder where you are,
I wish I may, I wish I might
(Stanley looks up and turns his head slightly.)
Oh brother! It's a satellite!

VENTRILOQUIST: That's awful! If I were your girl friend I'd give you poison.

STANLEY: If you were my girl friend, *I'd take it!*

Once a Blockhead, Always a Blockhead

VENTRILOQUIST: What a fine looking audience we have here. Look at all those bright and shining faces.

STANLEY: Yes, that lady has got a shiny nose.

VENTRILOQUIST: That's an insult. We have an audience here. How about saying "Hello" to them.

STANLEY: All right. HEL . . . LO AU . . . DIENCE!

VENTRILOQUIST: It would be better if you would say "Good evening, ladies and gentlemen."

STANLEY: Good evening, gentlemen and ladies.

VENTRILOQUIST: You have got the gentlemen before the ladies!

STANLEY: They usually are in *New York*!

VENTRILOQUIST: You are impossible!

STANLEY: No! I'm Stanley Higgins.

(Phone rings. Use a high metallic voice)

VENTRILOQUIST: Hello . . . *(pause)* . . . Yes, he's here.

(Put the phone up to Stanley's ear.)

STANLEY: Stanley Higgins here.

STANLEY: . . . . . . *(nods head)*

STANLEY: . . . . . . Is that so? *(laughs)*

STANLEY: Would you like to go out to a restaurant this evening?

VENTRILOQUIST: *(Do the phone vent voice as fast as you can as though the person on the other end of the line were arguing.)*

STANLEY: Well, if that's the way you feel about it, *good night*!

VENTRILOQUIST: What did your girl friend have to say when you asked her out to dinner?

STANLEY: She said, "I ain't going out with a blockhead like you!"

VENTRILOQUIST: It's not "I ain't going out." It's "I am not going out, you are not going out, she is not going out and we are not going out."

STANLEY: Ain't anyone going out?

VENTRILOQUIST: Where were you going to take her?

STANLEY: I was going to take her to the White Flower Inn.

VENTRILOQUIST: Why do they call it the White Flower Inn?

STANLEY: When you get the bill, your face turns *white*!

VENTRILOQUIST: You don't know much about girls, do you?

STANLEY: Only what I've been able to pick up.

VENTRILOQUIST: I thought you were a gentleman.

STANLEY: What's a gentleman?

VENTRILOQUIST: When a lady comes into a room, what are you supposed to do?

STANLEY: Whistle!

VENTRILOQUIST: No! When a lady comes into a room, you are supposed to tip your hat and bow. What does that show?

STANLEY: The *hole in my trousers*!

VENTRILOQUIST: If you are old enough to go chasing girls you are most certainly old enough to go to school. Do you go to school?

STANLEY: Oh yes . . . when I can't get out of it.

VENTRILOQUIST: What do you take at school?

STANLEY: Anything that isn't nailed down.

VENTRILOQUIST: That sounds like you steal. I don't like to hear that!

STANLEY: Well, you shouldn't listen then.

VENTRILOQUIST: Do you like your teacher?

STANLEY: She's all right, I suppose.

VENTRILOQUIST: What does she look like?

STANLEY: She looks like a saint.

VENTRILOQUIST: A saint?

STANLEY: Yes, a *Saint Bernard*!

VENTRILOQUIST: She doesn't.

STANLEY: Well, she barks at the kids all day long and bites her fingernails.

VENTRILOQUIST: Listen, now, here's a problem for you. If you have ten dollars in this pocket and ten dollars in the other one, what would you have?

STANLEY: Someone else's trousers!

VENTRILOQUIST: Spell the word "needle."

STANLEY: Needle. N . . . I . . . D . . . L . . . E.

VENTRILOQUIST: There's no "I" in needle!

STANLEY: How do you thread it then?

VENTRILOQUIST: What are you learning in Science, Stanley?

STANLEY: We are learning about air pollution.

VENTRILOQUIST: What are you doing to help prevent air pollution?

STANLEY: I stopped eating onions!

VENTRILOQUIST: *(Breathe heavily at dummy as you say:)* Pollution kills!

STANLEY: So does his breath!

VENTRILOQUIST: What do you think I could do to help prevent pollution?

STANLEY: Turn the *other way*!

VENTRILOQUIST: Ladies and gentlemen, I am going to sing "You Are My Sunshine."

STANLEY: *(tries to get off the ventriloquist's knee)* Oh . . . oh, here I go!

VENTRILOQUIST: Come back here *(pulls his coat a little)*. Why is it that every time I start to sing, you get up to leave?

STANLEY: *(to the audience)* I've heard him sing!

VENTRILOQUIST: That *is not very nice*!

STANLEY: *Neither is his voice!*

VENTRILOQUIST: I'll have you know that my voice sounds beautiful.

STANLEY: Yes, he sounds like a *sick cow*!

VENTRILOQUIST: "You Are My Sunshine."

STANLEY: Ohhhhhhhhhh! *(groans)*.

VENTRILOQUIST: What's wrong? Is my voice a little flat?

STANLEY: No, his head is though.

VENTRILOQUIST: "You Are My Sunshine."

STANLEY: *(shaking his head back and forth)* He really sounds sick!

VENTRILOQUIST: I'll have you know that my voice has been cultivated!

STANLEY: It *should have been plowed under*!

VENTRILOQUIST: *(singing)* "You'll never know, dear, how much I love you. Please don't take my sunshine away."

STANLEY: He still sounds sick!

VENTRILOQUIST: You don't understand. When I sing, I sing from the heart.

STANLEY: *(aside to audience)* If he had a heart, he wouldn't even sing.

VENTRILOQUIST: What makes you so stupid?

STANLEY: I don't know but whatever it is, *it works*!

VENTRILOQUIST: *(picking up the trick drinking glass)* I don't drink any more.

STANLEY: He doesn't *drink any less either*!

VENTRILOQUIST: I'm going to drink this glass of milk while you sing a song. *(Stanley nods his head back and forth.)*

STANLEY: That's what he thinks!

VENTRILOQUIST: Do you think I'm full of *bull*?

STANLEY: Yes sir, yes sir, three bags full! *(laughs)*

Drink the milk as explained on page 73.

VENTRILOQUIST: They're applauding for you, Stanley.

STANLEY: That's what you think!

VENTRILOQUIST: If they are not applauding then what are they doing?

STANLEY: They're hitting their hands against their faces to *stay awake*.

VENTRILOQUIST: Do you think that the audience learned anything from your singing?

STANLEY: Yes, *they learned that you can't sing*!

VENTRILOQUIST: That does it! You are going inside the suitcase!

You could finish the routine by placing your figure inside a suitcase.

VENTRILOQUIST: It's a funny thing, Stanley. All dogs, no matter how vicious, will wander up to me and lick my hand.

STANLEY: They might not be so friendly if you'd eat with a fork and knife.

STANLEY: Hurray. I've saved enough dough so we can go to Hawaii this summer.

VENTRILOQUIST: Great! When are we going to leave?

STANLEY: As soon as I save enough dough for us to get back.

VENTRILOQUIST: If you had 14 apricots and gave away 4, how many would you have left?

STANLEY: Ah, ahhhhh . . . I don't know. In my class we do math with apples.

For additional patter and jokes see Appendix C.

7. Giving a Stage Performance

THE TIME has now come to put together all the things you have learned and practiced, and introduce your partner to an audience.

Professional ventriloquists always exercise their voices before each performance. Practice the exercises for the tongue, the buzz and the drone while preparing to go on stage.

It is important that the audience never see the dummy while he is not moving and animated as this kills the illusion of life. Make him say a few words to the stage hands to get him into his personality before you go in front of the audience.

Most audiences react with excitement when the dummy and the ventriloquist make their entrance. "Isn't he sweet?" "Which one is the dummy?" Here are a couple of ways to create a lifelike appearance before any words are exchanged.

I sometimes make Stanley sneeze or follow a real or imaginary object as soon as he is seated on my knee. Jimmy Nelson, an American ventriloquist, makes Danny O'Day fall forward quickly and at the same time Danny yells "T-I-M-B-E-R!" and then the routine is started with the audience tuned in.

There are a variety of ways to position your figure once on stage. I prefer to place my foot upon a chair and then place Stanley on my knee. I always face the audience to prevent them from saying "He moved his head sideways so that we couldn't see his lips move." I make a compromise by turning my head slightly to the right and looking out of the corner of my eyes at my partner. If you stand while performing, you will be able to project your voice to a greater degree. For a smaller audience of 15 to 20 people, you could perform from a seated position. Some ventriloquists used to place their dummy on a suitcase that has been turned sideways. Others prefer to balance their figures on their left arm. Regardless of the position that you choose, it must feel comfortable and not look awkward.

Your partner should look at you when you are talking to him, then he might decide to look back at the audience to see what their reaction is. If a joke gets a good laugh, you should always wait until the laughter is at a low level before continuing the routine.

An old vaudeville saying is: If you present your routine *fast* enough and *loud* enough, it will be over before the audience has time to realize that it is poorly done!

Microphones

If the microphone goes dead, remember to stand in front of the curtain and project your voice as much as you can to prevent it from being absorbed by the curtains. To create a more natural impression the dummy should move closer to the microphone when he is speaking. I prefer to let the dummy use his own personal microphone, a broken tape recorder mike placed around his neck, which adds much realism to the presentation.

It is very important that the microphone stand be adjusted beforehand as the last performer on the bill might have been much taller and you would look very awkward trying to stretch your neck upward towards it. I usually ask the sound systems operator to adjust the microphone to the right volume and tone well in advance of the performance. This gives the voices maximum range and a pleasing tone color.

A person with a deep voice should advance the tone control towards the treble range and a person with a high voice could command greater attention from the audience if more bass tones were added. Since the tone color varies according to the type of system, its range and power, it is necessary to experiment beforehand to obtain the best possible sound.

The distance you should stand from the microphone varies according to the size of the amplifier and the sensitivity of the microphone. You can stand from 4 to 8 inches away from good quality equipment and still be heard in the back row of a theater.

The type of microphone used will depend upon the type of equipment used and the amount of movement in your routine. If a neck mike is used, you can manipulate the figure more freely without the voice fading out as you move out of the microphone's range.

Finally here are some tips gleaned from my experience in the public-speaking field.

(a) Don't touch the microphone, as this might muffle the sound or cause a screeching feedback type of sound.

(b) If the "p" and "t" sounds make an explosive popping noise over the speakers, speak into the microphone at an angle.

(c) The amplification system should emit a warm tone and not blast boisterously. An adult audience will tune out a blasting loud sound.

(d) If you have to clear your throat or cough, always turn away from the mike.

Remember, part of the success of your act will depend upon how well your comedy dialogue is communicated to your audience.

Venturing into television

Edgar Bergen and Charlie McCarthy gained world renown through network radio and television programs and were later awarded a citation for the variety program with the greatest listening audience in radio history. One of the reasons that Bergen attained success on the mass media is that he has perfected the "Four C's" of good speech; namely Correct pronunciation, Colorful and pleasing tone, Clear articulation and a Cultivated and Contemporary taste in humor. I suggest that the serious student of ventriloquism who wants to pursue a television or radio career should study speech from books or a qualified speech or dramatic teacher.

The old maxim "Experience is the best teacher" still applies to ventriloquism. As an amateur ventriloquist, you should first do shows for friends, benefits for charities, Boy Scout shows and church socials to get the publicity necessary for a chance with television. To get a spot on television, you must first sell your act to the program director. I usually send a neatly typed letter along with my most recent news clippings and brochures. You are likely to have more success if you ask for an audition in your letter as this gives you a chance to sell your sidekick's personality to the director. Children's shows and the interview variety shows seem to be the most popular type that play host to ventriloquists.

Another field that is being tapped by the creative performer is that of the television commercial. American and Canadian broadcasting companies have carried commercials by popular ventriloquists such as Shari Lewis and Cy Leonard.

Another way of obtaining a spot on television is to be discovered by a well known ventriloquist or show business personality who might take an interest in your act and help you to further your career. Sometimes large charity organizations hire celebrated personalities who might be willing to help you, if they feel that you have talent and personality.

Keep an eye open for organizations raising funds for charity needing talent, or churches or clubs holding special events.

The advance preparation that goes into a television program is most important. This idea was clearly illustrated to me while I was rehearsing for a children's show using Hossai the Mexican Rabbit, a handkerchief puppet. During the sound test trial, the boom operator complained that he was not picking up Hossai's voice very well. When I raised my head towards the microphone, I noticed that it was turned more towards Hossai while his voice was talking and the boom operator was probably deceived by the puppet's diffuse voice. He suggested that a neck clip-on mike would eliminate this difficulty and would also allow more movement during the routine.

Clothes

If the television program is in color, then your partner should wear his most flamboyant outfit. Reds and light blues show up to better effect than black and white. You should dress more conservatively so as not to detract from your partner's appearance. Any shiny pieces of equipment or jewelry should be avoided or powdered down to reduce the reflective glare.

Grooming

Good grooming is essential as the vigilant eyes of the camera will focus in on every detail.

The dummy's face and hands should be washed (shiny paints should be avoided as it will give the dummy an artificial appearance on television), the hair brushed and sprayed, the clothes dry-cleaned, and the shoes polished. A touch of glycerine could be added to the eyes to give him a more lifelike appearance. Remember, good grooming will help you to penetrate that invisible barrier in order to create a good rapport with your audience.

Routining your dialogue for television

Find out how much time you have been allowed and stick to it exactly. It is better to delete bits of business rather than deliver your dialogue too quickly. Most announcers pace their speech at about 100 words a minute; you should bear this in mind when pacing your dialogue. It should be built to captivate interest and attention from the word "go" and it should be climaxed with singing or your *best* joke.

If you are doing an interview type of show, you should have a short encore routine ready in case the host calls you back to have an informal chat with you and your partner. The host might even ask questions which you have previously given to him, neatly typed on a small card. Try to make your material revolve round the theme of the show or the personalities appearing on it. *Remember to use discretion in jokes with ethnic or religious overtones.*

HOST: Have you got a girl friend?
STANLEY: *(shyly)* No, not yet.
HOST: Well, what hobbies do you have to amuse yourself?
STANLEY: I like to hunt.
HOST: What kind of game do you hunt?
STANLEY: *Sexy blond chicks!*

Camera Capers

If the show is of the variety type, you should try to work out in advance the type of camera shots that would best highlight your act. If the program director sees your act beforehand he will suggest the different type of camera shots and how they could be used to best advantage. A close-up of the dummy alone will help to emphasize more emotional parts of the dummy's lines. The most commonly used shots are semi-close to medium range shots with an occasional profile shot of the dummy while he is crying or laughing. Profile shots of the ventriloquist might suggest to the viewers that this is being used to cover up your lip movement.

When you are introduced, walk on easily with a smile on your face. Walk gracefully to the performing position and make sure that the microphone is adjusted so that it is slightly lower than your mouth and on the same side that you manipulate your figure on.

If there is only a small studio audience present, you have to imagine that the camera is your best friend. When the red light comes on, try to get a personal tone into your voice as the home viewers are from 6 to 8 feet away from their sets. If the camera shots are not worked out beforehand, you will have to watch the red light and the monitor to make sure you are facing the correct camera.

Television offers a wide range of exciting opportunities for ventriloquists who are willing to perfect their voice manipulation, timing and lip movement.

8. Magic and Ventriloquism

What is magic?

Many of you might wonder what magic really consists of. Simply explained, it is the art of doing the impossible!

Magic is a series of moves presented in a special sequence by the performer who is an actor playing the part of a magician. At a certain point in the sequence, the audience's attention is distracted and a seeming miracle occurs.

A method commonly used by magicians to direct the audience's attention to an unimportant move in the sequence is called "misdirection." Here are some basic principles of misdirection that will help you to perform the magical effects explained in this chapter.

(a) The audience will look where you look.

(b) The audience will look where you point or verbally direct their attention.

(c) The audience's attention will be directed to bright colors, large quick movements and loud noises.

If tricks are shown in a dull and unconvincing manner, the audience will realize that it was the *device*, not the *deceptionist,* that fooled them. Add a touch of your personality to your effects to transform every "tiny trick" into a *miraculous feat.*

Magic and the Dummy

Like a magician, a ventriloquist makes use of many principles of misdirection. The illusion that his voice is coming from another source is aided by the manipulation of the dummy, and the greater the movement, the more the audience's attention will be directed away from the ventriloquist to the dummy.

Magic and ventriloquism can be combined very effectively into a whole new field of entertainment for the creative performer.

A simple trick, which can be obtained from most larger magic companies, is the color changing tie or flower effect. You could work this into the routine by suddenly noticing that the dummy's bow tie doesn't match his outfit and saying "That tie is so loud you should have a muffler with it." Your partner replies "Well, you're the magician, why not change it!" You change the color of his tie and he looks bewildered.

The Twentieth Century Silks

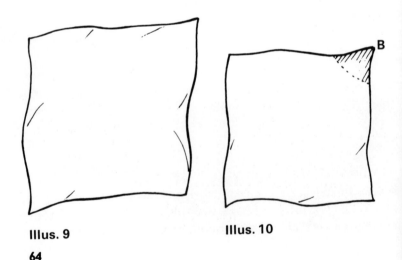

Illus. 9   Illus. 10

Illus. 11. As the coins appear they are dropped into the metal container with a clinking sound.

Illus. 12. Lo and behold—a shining coin makes its mysterious appearance.

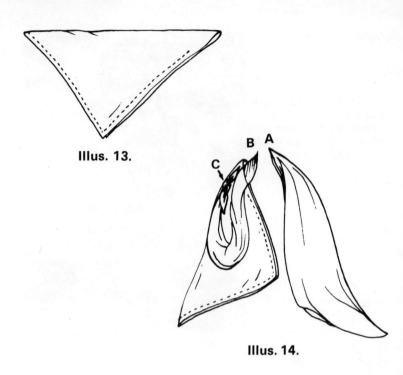

Illus. 13.

Illus. 14.

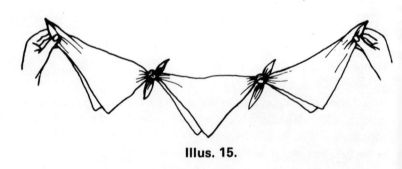

Illus. 15.

Preparation

1. A solid color 12″ blue silk (Illus. 9).

2. A multicolored silk with a blue corner (B) sewn on to the end (Illus. 10).

3. A second solid blue silk is folded diagonally (Illus. 13) and sewn around the outer open edges except for a small 2″ opening left for corner B to protrude from. The multicolored silk with the corner is placed through the opening in the blue sewn silk and is tied to the corner (see Illus. 14). The blue sewn-on corner should extend from the opening in the blue silk.

4. When silk A and B are tied together and given a slight shake, the multicolored silk will appear between the other two blue silks as in Illus. 15.

Two single silks are tied together, the knotted part being stuffed into the dummy's pocket. After a silk has disappeared mysteriously (see method below), the two tied silks are removed from your partner's pocket but to your embarrassment, there is still no multicolored silk in the pocket. When your partner has said a few magic words, you remove the handkerchiefs with a slight shake which exposes the vanished handkerchief tied between the other two.

This item can be bought from Tannen's Magic Co., 1540 Broadway, New York City, or from Mickey Hades Enterprises, Box 476, Calgary, Alberta.

How to make the silk vanish

As you show a multicolored silk, conceal in your hand a 3″ round cylinder type of pill container. In an up-and-down motion, your left thumb pushes the silk into the plastic pill container (Illus. 16). Place your hand into the dummy's pocket, but when you bring out your hand, palm the silk with the pill container. Your partner then leans forward, turns his head and asks, "What are those two blue handkerchiefs going to be

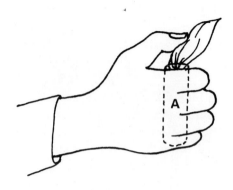

Illus. 16. The multicolor silk is pushed by the thumb into the plastic silk tube (A).

used for?" As your partner misdirects the audience's attention, you drop the pill container into your left side pocket.

Then you dramatically turn the dummy's pocket inside out to show it to be empty.

The Money from the Air or The Miser's Dream

Since many ventriloquists might not be familiar with the magical effect called The Miser's Dream, I shall explain in detail how to add this effect to your ventriloquist routine.

First of all, a pail is shown to be empty. Then the performer looks for an imaginary spot in the air. As his partner looks into the air, to his bewilderment, a shining coin suddenly makes its mysterious appearance (see Illus. 12). Coins then appear from behind the dummy's ear, in his nose, and from his mouth. As the coins appear they are dropped into the metal container with a clinking sound (see Illus. 17). As a climax to the routine, several coins cascade from the dummy's mouth amid the laughter and applause.

Illus. 17.

Since mechanical pails with coins concealed in the handles are very expensive if bought from a dealer, I have included a method which makes use of simple props such as metal flower pots and double-sided cellulose tape (Scotch tape).

Put a circle of double-sided cellulose tape around the forefinger of your left hand, leaving about a $1\frac{1}{4}''$ extension hanging down. Next attach a coin to the tape extension as shown in Illus. 18.

1. First show the pail with your free left hand, trying not to click the coin against the metal container as you pick it up.

2. As you reach into the air with the back of your hand towards the audience, the left thumb goes under the coin and

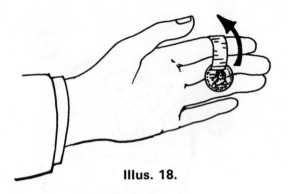

Illus. 18.

quickly flips it up to the position shown in Illus. 19. *Pause* to give everyone a chance to see the coin.

3. Then make a tossing motion towards the metal container. As your hand goes into the pail momentarily, you should clang the coin against the side of the pail and quickly withdraw the hand, allowing the coin to swing down into the position shown in Illus. 18. This move is repeated each time a coin is produced.

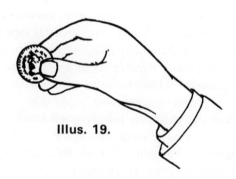

Illus. 19.

Illus. 20.

Remember, your partner should look very startled or surprised when the coins are being produced. After every 3 or 4 coins, he could come in with one of the following lines.

STANLEY: Money won't make you happy, but it is certainly good for quieting the nerves.

STANLEY: They say that money talks. The only thing it says to me is "Goodbye"! *(looks down into the waste can)* The cost of living is so high today, food is so expensive, it's cheaper to eat money, a-h-e-e-oh *(muffled tones)*.

You then extract several coins from your figure's mouth.

4. Reach up into the air for another coin but pretend that you are not able to catch one. As your partner laughs and starts to shake his head, let your hand fall to your left side to remove the coins from the holder, which is pinned under your suit (see Illus. 20). Next, bring your hand quickly in front of your partner's mouth and release your grip on the coins, gradually letting them cascade into the container. A few up-and-down movements of the dummy will add to the comedy of this presentation. He should speak in the muffled voice just before you remove the coins (see page 23).

Do not worry about the audience seeing you steal the coins from the holder as their attention will be directed towards the movements of your partner. All the above steps must be practiced until they blend into a smooth flowing routine.

Swami River, a comedy mind-reading routine

A comedy mind-reading act with a dressed-up figure would be very popular because of the interest in astrology and psychic phenomena. A turban could easily be made from a towel and a stone-studded pin could be attached to the front. To finish off the ensemble, an imitation mustache and goatee could be added with some surgical adhesive.

Once you have introduced your partner as the world-renowned mind reader, Swami River, you should have him blindfolded by the Master of Ceremonies or by a member of the audience. Here is a sample of the type of joke that you would use in your dialogue.

VENTRILOQUIST: Swami, tell me this fellow's name . . . for the love . . .

STANLEY: . . . Mike!

VENTRILOQUIST: What has this gentleman got around his neck?

STANLEY: . . . ah . . . ah . . . a collar!

VENTRILOQUIST: Absolutely correct! What color is it? Keep it clean . . .

STANLEY: White!

VENTRILOQUIST: Amazing!

If you should decide to use a comedy mind-reading act, you should exaggerate the movements of your figure slightly because he has been blindfolded.

Many ventriloquists find it difficult to entertain audiences of younger children because their gags and jokes are above the level of understanding of the children. To be successful with children you must be *flexible* and not stick to a rigidly fixed dialogue. Let your figure help out with your tricks. Let him sing songs and play games that the children are familiar with. In a nutshell, you should include anything that has movement, color, novelty and audience participation.

Children seem to be most enthusiastic when your partner successfully plays a joke on you. Try and visualize this scene. Your partner has a black tube in his hand (1½″ by 6″). He is holding it up to his eye, looking intently into it. Every once in a while he giggles and looks around to see if any one is watching him.

VENTRILOQUIST: Stanley, what are you looking at there?
STANLEY: W . . . O . . . W! Isn't she something!
VENTRILOQUIST: Can I look at her? *(excitedly)*.
STANLEY: Just look at those legs.
VENTRILOQUIST: Come on! Please let me look at her.
STANLEY: All right, I suppose you can.
VENTRILOQUIST: I can't see anything, Stanley.
STANLEY: Silly! Turn it around to focus the picture.
VENTRILOQUIST: I still can't see anything.
STANLEY: *I can! I can! (Stanley laughs at your black eye)*

The end of the paper tube has been coated with soot and when you turn it around against your eye, it gives you a ring of black like a black eye. The laughs in this routine are not obtained from jokes but by the comical situation with a *surprise* ending. This is a very old gag used with a new twist. Since it is completely visual it works with the youngest of audiences.

Drinking while singing

Many performers drink a glass of milk while their figures are singing or talking (see Illus. 22). Some use a mechanical glass for this stunt. The glass is built with a double wall with a small opening near the inner wall at the top. When you tilt the glass the liquid escapes through the opening to the inside of the inner shell. The illusion created is that the level of the milk has gone down.

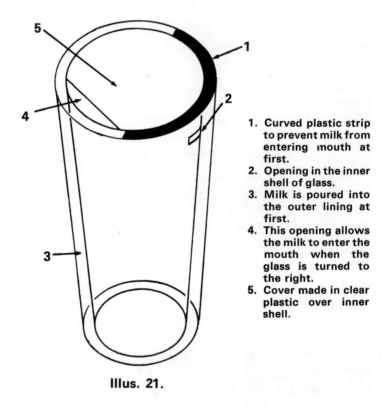

1. Curved plastic strip to prevent milk from entering mouth at first.
2. Opening in the inner shell of glass.
3. Milk is poured into the outer lining at first.
4. This opening allows the milk to enter the mouth when the glass is turned to the right.
5. Cover made in clear plastic over inner shell.

Illus. 21.

The milk does not enter your mouth at first as the top of the glass is partly sealed with a curved plastic strip as shown in Illus. 21. On the last note of the song, the glass is moved to the right so that the mouth is aligned with the opening.

On the last note of the song, the milk goes below your tongue which is curled slightly upwards to accommodate the milk. As you wipe your mouth with your handkerchief, swallow the milk. Combining trickery with skill enhances the illusion of drinking. When I have finished drinking, I always allow a drop or two of milk to spill on the floor to prove that the milk is not sealed in.

Illus. 22. While the ventriloquist appears to be drinking a glass of milk, the dummy is singing!

9. Adopting a Partner

NOWADAYS the wooden dummy is not so easy to buy and some ventriloquists are using hand puppets with moving mouths, which are far cheaper than dummies. You can also make these yourself, as explained later in this chapter.

However, if you are going to buy a dummy, there is no need to get a very expensive one to start with. It is only really necessary to have the basics to create a lifelike impression—a moving head, a moving mouth and a lever to turn the eyes sideways.

You should buy a figure that has different facial features from your own as this will create a better contrast. You should also try to tailor the personality of your dummy to his actual appearance. A young looking figure might play the part of a wisecracking schoolboy. This type of personality might like to brag and show off a lot, and he will most certainly love to interrupt when the ventriloquist is speaking.

Suppliers of dummies are listed in Appendix D.

How to make a carrying case

Having invested money on a figure, it is important to protect your investment so that it is not easily damaged while being carried from show to show. A sponge-lined cloth bag with a draw-string at the bottom will help to protect the finish of the head.

You should buy a semi-trunk suitcase, preferably one made of lightweight metal. Three-eighths of an inch plywood sections could be screwed in as in Illus. 23 (3). A small belt could be attached, as in (2), in order to hold the dummy secure.

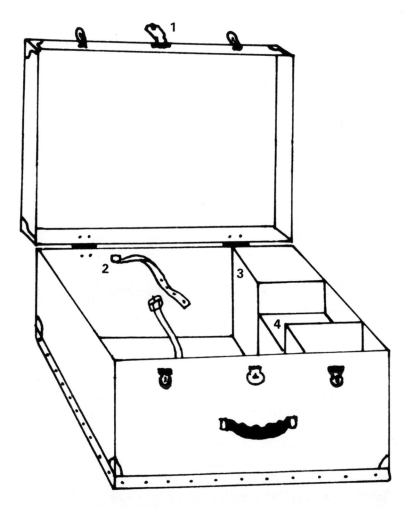

Illus. 23. 1. Lock for the case. 2. Canvas belt to hold dummy secure. 3. Plywood insert lined with spongy material. 4. Dummy's head fits into this section, which is also lined with sponge-like material.

Rabbit Puppet

For this, you need a plain handkerchief, a strip of Velcro and some felt. (Velcro consists of two strips of material, which, when pressed together, make a firm bond.)

The features for the face and the bow tie are cut out of felt, as in Illus. 24. Glue one strip of the Velcro on to the backs of each cut out for the face, and attach a piece of elastic to the bow tie.

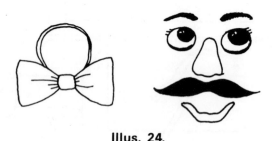

Illus. 24.

Stick the other strip of Velcro to the handkerchief (look at Illus. 25). Place the handkerchief over your hand with the Velcro outside and level with your two middle fingers. Tuck the handkerchief in a little between your fingers at X and Y. Bring corner A round and tuck it in at X, pulling the end through about 2 inches. Bring corner B down to Y in the same way. This makes the rabbit's ears.

Hold your hand as in Illus. 26 and tuck the excess material in at C.

Now put the bow tie around your wrist and attach the cutouts to the Velcro on the handkerchief.

To animate the puppet, simply move the fingers up and down about $\frac{3}{4}$ inch.

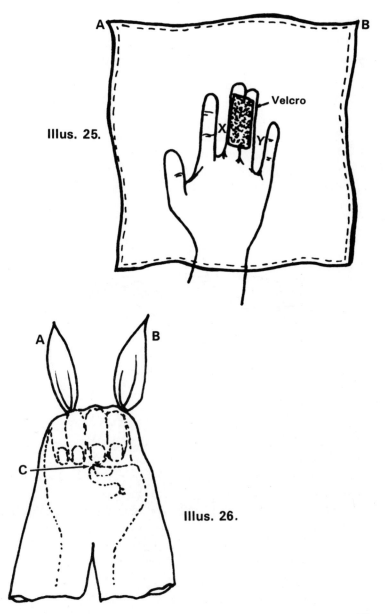

Illus. 25.

Velcro

Illus. 26.

79

Gertrude the talking cow

This puppet can easily be made out of heavy cardboard or plywood. Here is a list of some of the things that you will need:

1. 9″ × 9″ piece of quarter-inch plywood.
2. A dowel—6″ cut from an old broomstick will do.
3. Five small screw eyelets, two ¾″ screws.
4. Some old scrap material and a ring of metal.
5. ½″ bolt and nut, two washers.
6. Some elastic cord one foot along.

(a) Cut out the cow pattern leaving out the mouth (shaded in C, Illus. 27).

Illus. 27.

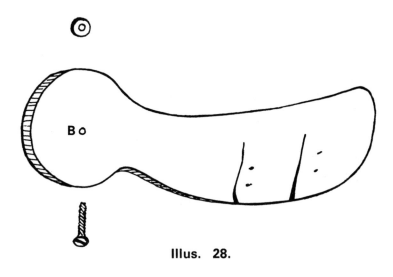

Illus. 28.

(b) Cut out a separate mouth (Illus. 28).

(c) Attach mouth behind wooden cutout and fasten with a bolt, nut and washers at B (Illus. 28).

(d) Attach the dowel with $\frac{3}{4}''$ screws at D (Illus. 29).

(e) Place screw eyelets on the back of cow according to their position in Illus. 29.

(f) Attach elastic cord to all of the eyelets as shown in Illus. 29.

(g) Tie a ring on the end of the elastic cord at point E on Illus. 29.

(h) Tack or glue colored cloth around the base of the cutout to hide the manipulation stick. Stuffed arms could be added as well. See the hand-puppet pattern for directions on how to make the stuffed arms.

(i) Paint the cow in brown and white matt paint. Black paint could be used to highlight the markings on the face.

(j) Bits of hair and felt could be added to give this profile puppet a more realistic appearance.

To operate Gertrude you merely curl your fingers around the dowel and slip your thumb through the ring, pulling the ring once for each mouth movement. These profile puppets are also effective in shadow plays as they have a moving mouth and a distinct profile.

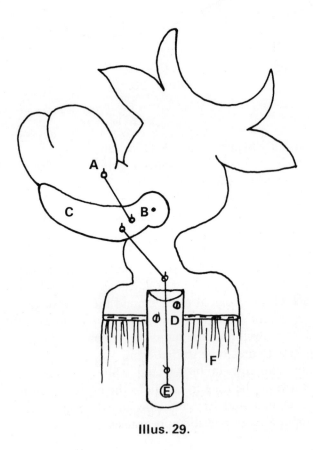

Illus. 29.

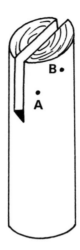

Illus. 30. This 6-inch dowel has a $\frac{1}{4}$-inch groove at the top to accommodate the cut-out of the cow's head. Put two screws in, at A & B.

Bozo the Clown

(an easy-to-make paper bag puppet)

To make Bozo the Clown, take a small paper bag, about $3'' \times 6''$ or $4'' \times 8''$. Fold the bag flat along the creases as shown in Illus. 31. Next, round the top of the bag off, being careful not to cut the complete top section off (see A). Cut the folded-over part of the bag up at B and C (about $\frac{1}{2}''$). This flap, which allows for lip movement, should be $2''$ long. Make a cone-shaped hat for Bozo and glue it to the front of the bag.

Glue on some red wool or curled paper strips for hair. A fancy paper doily could be used for the frilly part of the clown's costume. Paint the face in white and then add a red mouth and big black eyes and a wadded-up tin foil ball for a nose. To move Bozo's mouth, simply place your thumb below the fold at the front and the rest of the fingers above the fold inside the bag.

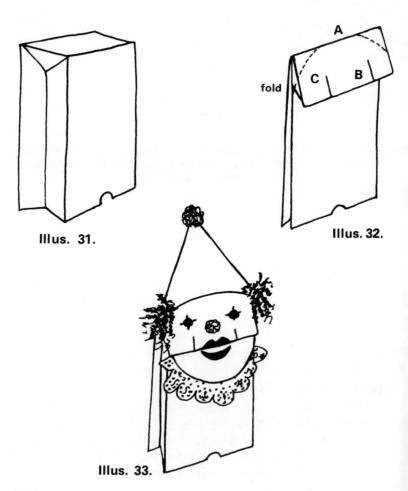

Illus. 31.

Illus. 32.

Illus. 33.

Illus. 34.

Rabbit and dog bag puppets

You will notice that these designs are larger than the previous one as the cutouts extend beyond the paper bag. Stiff Bristol board or corrugated cardboard should be used for the head and body. Basic steps for this larger puppet are:

Illus. 35. Dog bag puppet.

Illus. 36. Mouth of dog puppet.

A

li

1. Trace desired pattern onto cardboard sheet.
2. Cut out head and body separately.
3. Place the upper lip of the head along the fold of the bottom of the bag and then firmly glue it in place.
4. Next, glue the body to the front of the bag under the fold.
5. Next take a red piece of construction paper and fold it in half and then place it under the fold at A. Bend the paper that protrudes above and below the fold in the bottom of the bag.
6. Cut a lip design on the folded-over part of the red strip and cut it out, and finally glue mouth inside the fold of the bag.
7. Finish with yarn for hair, bits of scrap felt for eyes.
8. Arms of the rabbit and dog are simply double construction paper with pipe cleaners glued in between.

Socky the hound

To make Socky the Hound, take an old sock and lay it flat on the table with the heel facing upward. Put your hand into the sock and mark the spot with chalk where your hand joins your thumb. (See the arrow on Illus. 37.) Then cut around the edge of the sock with good sharp scissors up to your chalked mark (see Illus. 38). *Don't* cut across the sock. The front part that you have cut will become Socky's mouth. Now take some heavy red cardboard (5″ × 5″) and fold it in half and then place the folded end inside the slit in the sock as shown in Illus. 39. Next, trace around the edge to obtain your pattern as shown in Illus. 39. Finally, cut the traced pattern out and it will resemble Illus. 40.

Place the mouth into the front cut of the sock evenly. Finally, put all-purpose glue on the *outer* edge along the slit in the sock (Illus. 41). To prevent frayed edges, turn in the glued edge of the sock about $\frac{1}{4}″$ and press evenly to the edges of the cardboard mouth.

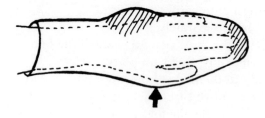

Illus. 37.

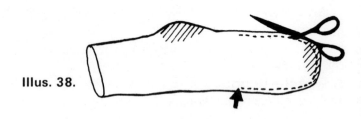

Illus. 38.

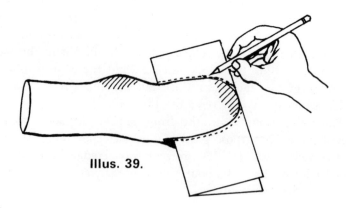

Illus. 39.

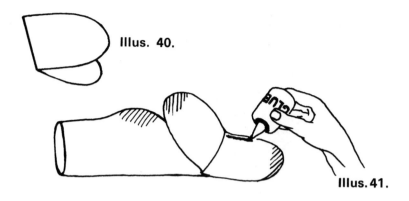

Illus. 40.

Illus. 41.

Put several heavy books on top of the mouth and the sock until the glue is thoroughly dry. To make Socky come to life, buttons or Teddy-bear eyes and a pom-pom made of wool could be sewn on as in Illus. 42.

Long, flappy ears could be cut out of felt to match the sock and then glued or sewn as depicted in Illus. 42.

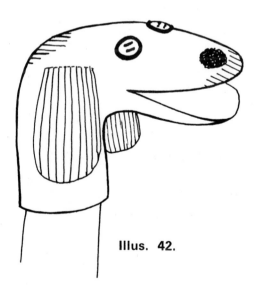

Illus. 42.

Paper Plates Puppet

1. Fold a paper plate in half as shown in Illus. 43.

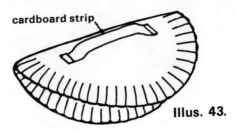

cardboard strip

Illus. 43.

2. Staple a cardboard strip to the top and the bottom of the plate. These strips aid in the movement of the mouth. In operation, four fingers are inserted in the top strip and the thumb is placed in the bottom strip.

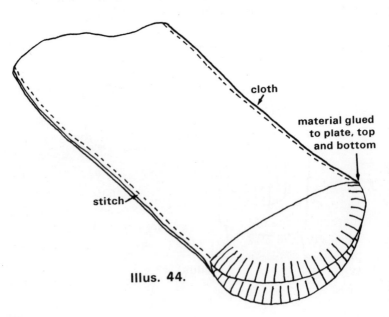

cloth

material glued to plate, top and bottom

stitch

Illus. 44.

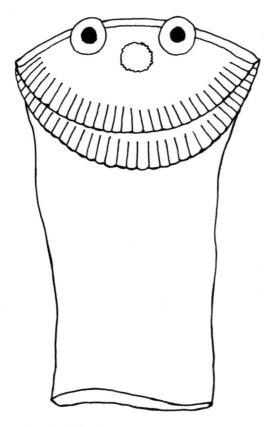

Illus. 45. Finished paper plates puppet.

3. Take two pieces of cloth, each 1 foot in length and the width of the paper plate. Glue the short end of one piece of material to the top edge of the plate as shown in Illus. 44. Then glue the other piece of material to the bottom of the plate in a similar manner.
4. When the glue has dried, stitch along both lengths with thread.

5. Next glue the eyes and the nose on. Old scrap pieces of felt could be used for a nose or a tongue. Shiny buttons could be used for the eyes. Bits of wool could be used to add some hair to our friend.

If you haven't a paper plate, a wooden match box could be cut in half as shown in Illus. 46 and 47. Attach the cloth in the same manner and then decorate the puppet.

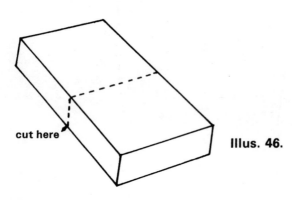

cut here

Illus. 46.

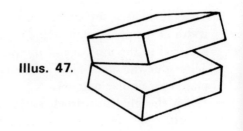

Illus. 47.

Pattern for Boy or Girl Puppet

Remember to cut the slash in the mouth. Put the cardboard inside and glue all around the edge of it. Next stick the edge of the mouth all around the edge of the cardboard. Finally stick the red cloth mouth over the rough edges on the outside.

Black wool could be used for hair. Flannel or any other heavy material could be used for the puppet. Clothes could be made from bits of material and buttons.

The fingers could be glued and then sewn on the outside by machine. The hands and the ears could be stuffed with bits of cut-up nylons or other scrap material.

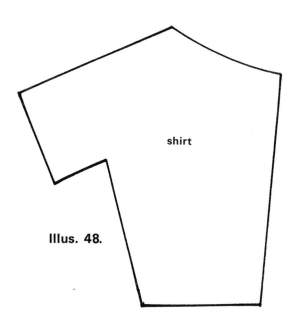

shirt

Illus. 48.

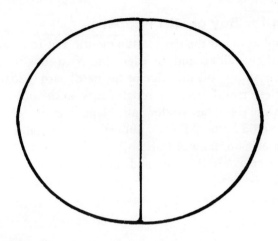

Illus. 49. Mouth folds along middle line. You need two mouths, one in red material and one in cardboard for backing red material.

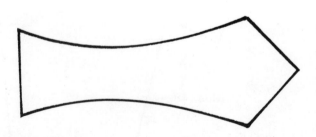

Illus. 50. Tie for boy puppet.

Illus. 51. Hand. Cut out 4 hand patterns. Glue ends of fingers of each pair together. Stuff with cut-up nylons.

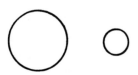

Illus. 52. Eyes. Cut out two large white discs and two smaller black ones (or you could use old Teddy-bear eyes).

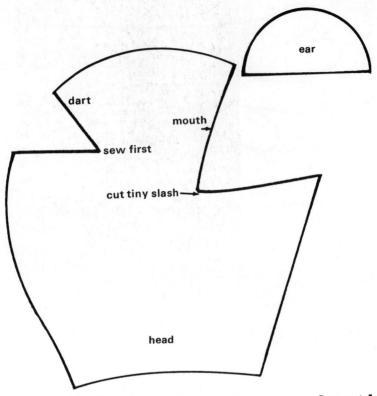

Illus. 53. Head. Cut out two head patterns. Ears-Cut out 4.
Sew ear to head by hand.

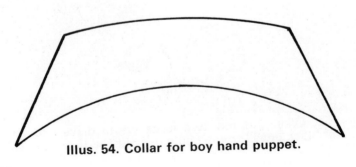

Illus. 54. Collar for boy hand puppet.

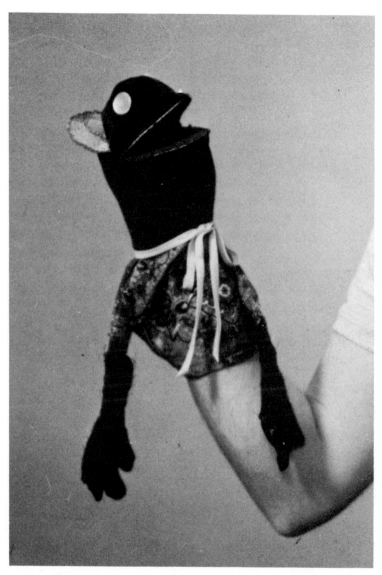

Illus. 55. An animal variation on the Boy and Girl Puppet Pattern.

Let Your Fingers Do the Talking: A Mouse Puppet

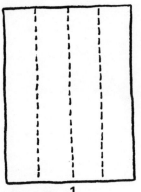 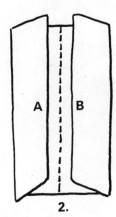 

Illus. 56.

1. Take the piece of paper and fold it in half lengthwise and then open it.
2. Fold A and B even with the middle crease and then leave the paper closed.
3. Next fold the right half over to the left side of the paper.

Illus. 57.

 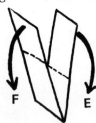 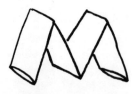

4. Then fold C up onto D.
5. Fold all layers of the top flap down to meet the center fold as shown in E and F. It should resemble a giant letter M.
6. Insert your fingers into the top pocket and your thumb into the bottom pocket, as depicted in Illus. 58.

6.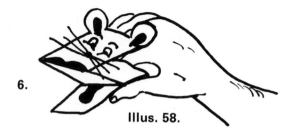

Illus. 58.

7. Glue on the pipe-cleaner whiskers, and then add the felt ears, eyes etc.

8. As a final realistic touch, attach a cardboard body with felt cutouts to the underside of the mouth.

9. A lead pencil taped to the back of the right leg will make the puppet dance when the pencil is rolled between your forefinger and thumb.

Illus. 59.

The Little Old Man Figure

If you can't afford to buy one of the more elaborate wooden carved dummies, then here is a compact figure which is easy to construct.

Materials

1. One piece of $\frac{3}{8}''$ plywood $12'' \times 24''$; $\frac{3}{8}''$ ply $9'' \times 4''$ base (D).
2. Scrap bits of felt and imitation hair and mustache.
3. Two spring-hinged levers.
4. Four $\frac{3}{8}''$ wood screws.
5. Two small flaps in $\frac{1}{4}''$ plywood (approx. eye flap $2\frac{1}{2}'' \times 6''$; mouth $2\frac{1}{2}'' \times 3''$).
6. A few dozen $\frac{1}{4}''$ shoe tacks for attaching the clothes to the basic framework.
7. Some white glue and pipe cleaners for spectacles.
8. Flesh-colored and black paint and fine brush $\frac{1}{4}''$ size.

Directions

1. Draw wooden framework as depicted in Illus. 61 and cut out and sand.
2. Nail $9'' \times 4''$ base to the bottom of the framework (see D on Illus. 61).
3. Cut out slot for the mouth and the openings for the eyes.
4. Paint the eyes and the bottom lip on the flaps so that they are positioned as shown in Illus. 61.
5. Attach flaps with $\frac{3}{8}''$ screws so that the flaps can slide freely.
6. Attach spring hinges as shown in A and B in Illus. 61.
7. Attach stuffed felt arms to C as in Illus. 60 and then tack legs to the base at D.
8. Glue the glasses, mustache, tie, hair, etc. after the face and hands have been painted in dull flesh color.
9. Small cloth sneakers could be stitched onto the end of the trousers.

Attaching the Mouth

1. Cut the mouth flap in half and tack each piece of plywood to a small block of $\frac{3}{8}''$ as shown in Illus. 62, part B.

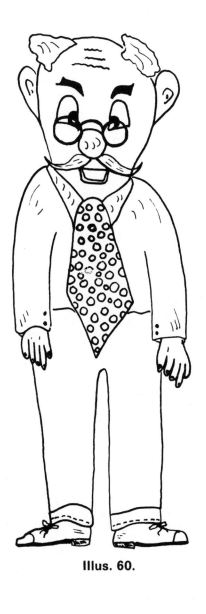

Illus. 60.

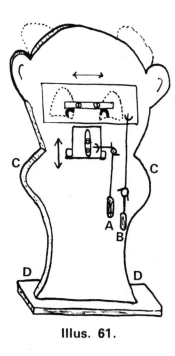

Illus. 61.

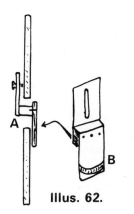

Illus. 62.

2. Paint the non-slotted part of the flap in flesh and then add the lip as shown in B.
3. Place the mouth flap through the opening in puppet framework as depicted in Illus. 61.
4. Finally place screws in slot to enable the mouth to slide up and down easily.

To animate your figure, move lever A to move mouth up and down. By manipulating lever B side eye movement can be achieved. Remember, your friend has a little touch of rheumatism, so please, not too many fast movements.

A Daily Practice Routine

Many professional ventriloquists spend more time learning new dialogues instead of reviewing the fundamental principles of ventriloquism. If you desire to attain a higher level of skill in ventriloquism you should practice every day for at least one hour. (2 half-hour sessions.)
1. Do the breathing exercises 1, 2, and 3 on pages 13–15.
2. Do all of the tongue exercises mentioned earlier on page 12.
3. Practice the vowels a, e, i, o, u in the "slay" tone.
4. Next say the complete alphabet in the "slay" tone.
5. Make up a list of single words that you find difficult to say and go over them every day in the "seay" tone.

baby	fun	money	Peter	tea	value
Betsy	forest	more	panting	tough	vest
father	house	Miss	piston	taxes	vast
fudge	hill	Mary	pallid	tailor	way
fair	many	Pop	poster	very	Willy
					you

6. Next practice sentences with many difficult letters in them.
   Big black baby buggy bumpers.
   Peter Piper picked a peck of pickled peppers.
   Sister Susie sold seashells on the sea shore on Sunday.

Many men might master more money.
Try making some sentences yourself!

7. Read alternate lines from a book or newspaper.
8. Finally practice your routine in pantomime in front of a mirror.

   (a) Then practice dialogue with sound.

   (b) Next practice without a mirror.

   The mirror is an aid in improving manipulation.
9. As a final step in improving your routine, have a friend tape your act in front of a live audience. Listening to the tape carefully will help you remove the poor laugh-getters from your dialogue. As every audience response to humor is different, the taping should be done on several occasions before removing any material from your routine.

Illus. 63. Stanley in his smart carrying case.

10. The Professional Touch— Music

WHETHER amateur or professional, you should attempt to add lively music to your present act to make it more up-to-date. If a band or pianist is not present, a good quality tape-recorded musical introduction is very effective as it creates excitement prior to and during your entrance. After you enter and walk smartly to front center stage and position your partner, the music volume could be faded out slowly. A local orchestra, for a small fee might let you tape a live musical introduction. Sometimes sound-effect records include good musical introductions that could also be taped.

Many ventriloquists sing in their acts, as experience has taught them that audiences believe that it is more difficult to sing than talk. For this reason every ventriloquist should add singing to his act. Modern folk songs and popular songs with a beat seem to be most popular. "This Land Is Your Land," and "Supercalifragilisticexpialidocius" and "Spoonful of Sugar" are all excellent songs as they have a rousing rhythm. You should try to relate the song to the theme of your routine. A cowboy-oriented dialogue would be best combined with a country-and-Western song may be with some yodeling. (Example: Wilf Carter—"My Little Yoho Lady".) On the other hand, gospel-oriented dialogues might be best suited for songs like "Man from Galilee" and "Michael" or any other popular hymn that could be related to your message.

If there is no recorded or live music available, start the audience clapping in time with the song, as this provides an an excellent audience participation finish to your act. If you perform in large theaters and night club settings, you should have specially scored music. The local musician's union will help to secure the services of a good music arranger. The arranger will score the music in the most suitable key and will advise you with regard to the placement of cues in the music. The music should be scored in such a manner to enable it to sound right if less than a complete orchestra is used. Many times you will only have piano, bass and drums. In larger night clubs in Las Vegas, a minimum arrangement for 12 pieces would be: conductor, piano, drums, bass, first trombone, first, second, third trumpet, first and second tenor saxophone, and first and second alto saxophone. The master-scored music sheet will then have to be copied for the 12 different parts and this of course will be an additional expense. Try to keep the music simple with a small number of cues to enable part-time musicians to do a presentable job with little or no rehearsal.

11. In the Limelight

BEFORE electricity was used extensively in theaters, a lime and oxygen compound was burned and used in spotlights or "limelights." This probably explains the origination of the term, "being in the limelight."

Poor lighting can ruin the impact of a good act, but good lighting can make a mediocre act look more professional. Understanding the principles that govern good lighting will enable you to attain the best possible lighting for your act. Good lighting should separate the performer from the background, producing a three-dimensional effect. Secondly, if the light is to appear natural it should have a main or "key" source of light coming from a 40- to 60-degree angle above the performer and this source of light should create a set of natural shadows.

The key light (A) should be placed at an angle of 45 degrees left of the performer and should come from above as it is the customary sun angle by which most objects are viewed outside. See Illus. 64.

The fill light (B) is now placed on the right side to soften the shadows produced by the key light. The fill light should not be as high as the key light and should be twice as far from the performer if the same intensities of bulbs are used. By carrying two photoflood adjustable stands with two 200-watt reflectors, you can transform a dully lighted performing area into a professionally lighted one. Never use footlights unless you use a strong-intensity spotlight with them as it tends to give you and your partner's face a rather cadaverous appearance.

Illus. 64.

In large theaters or night clubs where professional lighting is available, you should try to gear the lighting to suit the mood of your dialogue. If your partner is in a melancholy mood, the lights could be dimmed or filtered to blue.

If you wish to create a chilled, ghostly atmosphere, a green spotlight is very effective. Finally, to create a greater contrast between the performer and the audience, the house lights should be turned out or dimmed before your entrance; this tends to have a calming effect upon the audience and serves to focus attention on the performer in the limelight. The overall impression created by your act will be enhanced by well balanced lighting.

12. Publicity on Parade

IN ORDER to become known as a prospective ventriloquist you should explore the ever-varying array of techniques used by promoters and advertising men to publicize performers. One way to imprint your name and your partner's in the minds of the audience is to have a photograph with good contrast enlarged into a poster. If prominently displayed at your place of performance, it would not only add an air of professionalism to your entertainment but would also help to fix your name in the minds of the audience.

Business cards professionally printed are another way of promoting your "vent" act. Don't be stingy—hand out a large supply to key people after each performance. The card should include your name and your partner's name, the fact that you are a ventriloquist and finally your phone number and address. A small cartoon or symbol could be incorporated if it doesn't crowd the card and cheapen it. Experience has taught me that many people lose or discard business cards as they have no immediate use for them. Calendars, word puzzles, and optical illusions printed on the reverse side of the card create permanent interest in them. Here is an intriguing word puzzle that I have used on my own calling cards. Have the message shown in Illus. 65 printed on the back of your calling cards.

As a beginner in ventriloquism you should perform at several private parties in order to publicize your act. After you attain sufficient publicity, it will be necessary for you to set a fee if the audience is to truly appreciate your talent. The fee that you receive is usually based on how well known you are, your confidence and experience, the budget of the person

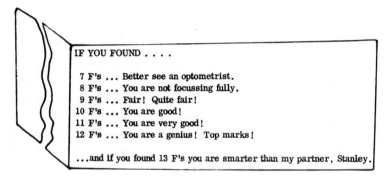

Illus. 65.

hiring you and the financial status of the area in which you are performing. Some performers set their fees according to the length of the act and transportation is an additional charge. Good amateur vents can net from $35 to $75 per show and on the other hand a professional who is well known can receive $150 to $1,500 per show. The old adage; if they pay for it, they think it's good, is still an excellent rule to adhere to when approached to do a benefit show.

If you decide to turn professional, earning a living solely from ventriloquism, a full-time agent is a distinct advantage. If, on the other hand, you are a semi-professional, it is not essential to have an agent, as many small-time agents do very little to promote and publicize your act. The best type of advertising by far is by word of mouth, as it is inexpensive and very effective in producing results. If you don't have an agent and still want to display an air of professionalism, a mimeographed or printed contract form should be sent to all persons booking your act. There is a sample of the contract form with all of the essential requirements in Illus. 66.

Two copies of this contract form should be sent via first class mail to the entertainment chairman along with other brochures or posters that you might have. Past experiences have demonstrated that telephone bookings without a confirmed written contract can result in misunderstandings concerning time of show or the fee charged.

Ventriloquism is not only a medium of entertainment but a prolific tool of communication in the fight against accidents, crime, drug abuse and other contemporary problems that perplex society. You will find it much easier to obtain comprehensive coverage from radio, press and television if you occasionally present a meaningful message along with the vent dialogue. Since ministers of the Gospel have used ventriloquism successfully to sell their messages, there is no reason why psychologists, speech teachers, policemen and others could not convey their ideas more emphatically through ventriloquism.

I have tried to give you some of the techniques used by promoters and agents to obtain publicity. The publicity and the fee that you receive will depend directly upon the success with which you apply these techniques to practical situations.

please sign and return. C O N T R A C T A G R E E M E N T ,
one copy of this form.

    between: Darryl Hutton and Stanley,covering an appearances at

the _Steelworkers Hall_ , in _Cambridge_

on _December 20, 75_ (date) at _3.00 pm._ (showtime)

Booker's name and address _Massey Fergus_

Booker's phone number is _658-9194_

How to get to place of performance _Turn right at_
second light, past water street bridge
and is on corner of King and Grand Ave.

The _steel local 246_ agrees to pay the artist,Darryl Hutton
and Stanley the sum of:

CHECK THE FEE OF YOUR CHOICE:

◯ 10 minutes   ◯ 20 minutes   ◯ 30minutes
  $250.00 $500.00 $750.00

         Performer _Darryl Hutton & Stanley_

         Booker _Massey Fergus_ .

Illus. 66.

13. Ventriloquism and Speech Correction

VENTRILOQUISM can be used to good effect in helping children with speech difficulties.

Speech fright is almost the same as stage fright, only the latter is outwardly shown as an inability to speak before a group of people because of fear caused by lack of security.

First of all, you should structure opportunities like story-telling so that the child can express himself orally. You should also let the child know that if he keeps on trying he will soon overcome the fear of speaking in front of an audience.

Then, let your student put on a puppet show from behind a stage so that he can project his personality into the puppet without being seen directly by the audience. Later, when the child gains more confidence, he could manipulate a larger figure with more movements. As the child practices with the dummy, he will become so preoccupied with its manipulation that he will forget his fear of speaking in front of an audience. After all, the dummy is really speaking!

Most of the minor speech difficulties fall into the category of the "lazy tongue," which is an inability to make the correct sounds because of faulty learning at an early age. These speech patterns unconsciously become reinforced by parental approval at an early age and through constant use they develop into hard-to-break habits.

If articulation is not right for boys by 8 years of age and girls by $6\frac{1}{2}$, it is retarded. If the speech is defective before these ages it is usually called "baby talk."

If the child is extremely shy, the sound imitations below could be done with a hand puppet with a moving mouth so that the attention is not directly on the child until the shyness barrier is partially broken.

Below are four of the main ways in which speech fright and the "lazy tongue" manifest themselves in children.

1. Any defect of hearing.
2. Stuttering, stammering or any hesitations in speech.
3. Lisping—any difficulty with sibilants—using 'th' for 's'.
4. Infantile speech-letter substitution—using one consonant for another (tome and do—come and go)

Exercises to develop power of stream of breath are essential in the production of many consonant sounds.

This is why good breathing in ventriloquism is a real asset toward the development of good speech.

Things to practice
blowing a feather of strips of paper;
blowing in hand to feel the air;
blow and say h-h-h-h-h-h-h-h-h-h.

P (an engine puffing or a motor boat)
Close your lips lightly, and as you open them suddenly, let the breath escape with a slight puff.

B (same as "P" with voice)
Imitate a baby babbling. Close your lips lightly; open suddenly with a vibration of vocal cords. Never give this sound without a vowel following it. (bu or bah)

M (imitate a humming top)
Block your mouth by closing your lips with your teeth slightly separated. The breath escapes through your nose with the vibration of the vocal cords.

W (imitate the wind)
Lips are slightly more rounded than for "oo." Expel the air with the vibration of the vocal cords.

H (imitate a dog panting "h-h-h-h-h")

Your mouth is open and the "h" is produced by the emission of the breath in a continuous stream through the vocal cords, causing friction but not vocalization.

T (imitate a ticking watch)

Press the tip of your tongue against the teeth ridge. Drop your tongue suddenly, letting air escape with an explosive sound.

D (imitate the sound made by a dove)

It is produced with your tongue in somewhat the same position as for "t" with voice added.

N (imitate the sound of sawing wood)

Place the front edge of your tongue against the teeth ridge. The vocal cords vibrate as the breath escapes in a continuous stream through the nose.

K Try to cough up an imaginary bone.

G This is the same as "K" but with voice added. Try to imitate a frog.

J This sound is the same as a "ch" with voice or said to be produced by a combination of "d" and "z." Imitate some bells ringing.

NG Also imitate a bell ringing but say ding-dong very slowly.

Y This is the sound that a pig makes when his tail is pulled (like a long "ee" sound).

F (imitate a spitting cat)

Bite your lower lip and then blow.

V This sound is made like a "f" voiced. Bite your lip and make a buzzing sound.

TH This is a voiced sound as in "they." Bite your tongue and make a buzzing sound.

SH (imitate the sound for "Be quiet"—sh-sh)

You could also imitate the driving of some chickens out of a garden. "Shoo! Shoo!"

L (imitate a bell ringing)

Place the front of your tongue on the teeth ridge and say "l." Don't curl your tongue back too far. For drill say "lah, lah, lah" which makes the tongue move very quickly.

S (imitate a snake, steam from a kettle or a goose)
With teeth almost closed, blow through your teeth with a soft hissing sound. (Hold your tongue well up behind the teeth.)

Z This sound is simply a voiced "s" sound. Imitate some bees buzzing.

R (imitate a growling dog)
Young children often substitute "w" for "r" by using lips instead of tongue to form "r." For "r" the lips are kept still and relaxed. The sides of the tongue are raised as when saying the vowel "ee" and the front of the tongue is raised toward the teeth ridge without touching it.
Put your hand on your throat to feel the vibration of the vocal cords when "r" is produced.

TH This TH sound is voiceless, as in "thumb." You should bite your tongue and blow. Imitate an angry goose.

CH This sound is produced by the combination of "t" and "sh." Try to imitate an engine—choo-choo.

THR Say "th," pull your tongue in quickly and say "r" (th - - r -).

You should practice the sounds which require the articulation of the tip of the tongue with the teeth ridge: t, d; s, z; and l. It is important that the tip of the tongue does not touch the upper teeth.

Substitutions

Never let a child practice for long periods of time as this might put stress on his or her vocal cords.

COMMON SUBSTITUTIONS	SIMPLE TEST
t for k	Come and go.

d for g	Come and go.
p for f	Four and five.
t for s	Six and seven.
th for s	Six and seven.
w for l	Light the lamp.
f for th-in	I hurt my thumb.
s for th-in	I hurt my thumb.
f for thr	I saw three boys.
d for th-ey	I saw them there.
w for r	Ring around a rosy.
l for r	Ring around a rosy.
b for v	It is very warm.
v for w	It is very warm.
Omitting the s in sp	Bring me a spoon.
sm	Smell the smoke.
sk	Skip and skate.
sw	Can you swim?
sn	See the snow.
st	Stop at the store.
Omitting the l in pl	Please play.
bl	Black and blue.
cl	Clean gloves.
gl	Clean gloves.
fl	See the flags.
sl	Don't slide on the floor.

Before you administer the informal speech test you should encourage the child to speak spontaneously with his puppet. If a child pronounces a word incorrectly or substitutes one consonant for another, don't reprimand him or exhibit any anxiety. When the child is speaking freely, with mistakes, have the child read orally the sentences on the right-hand side of the speech test while you circle the substitutions as you detect them.

After you determine the substitutions that the child is

experiencing difficulty with, you should demonstrate to the student the position of the tongue by manipulating the felt tongue of the animal hand puppet. If the pupil has trouble with the "R" sound, I would explain and show the position of the tongue and then read aloud a short story incorporating the sound that the child has difficulty with. For this sound I would probably read orally the fable, "The Dog and His Shadow," and at the part in the story where the dog growls, the pupil would make a g-r-r-r-r-r-r, g-r-r-r-r-rrrr sound with his dog hand puppet.

The use of puppets in speech correction not only captivates and holds the student's attention, but also removes self-consciousness from the child by directing attention away from the child toward the puppet. Constant praise and encouragement given to the child will help to reinforce the newly learned speech habits.

Does your voice carry well ?

Do you get a little hoarse after finishing several shows? Do you have trouble being heard when the microphone breaks down? If you have to answer any of the above questions in the affirmative then you have experienced difficulty with the projecting of your voice without enough support.

Ventriloquism is an asset to anyone who has to speak publicly as it enhances tonal quality and articulation and increases the distance that the voice will be carried. Carefully following the series of drawings that follow will enable you to improve the projection level of your voice.

The Steam Kettle Exercise

Take a short sip of breath and, as you let the air out slowly, hiss in a thin stream, through your teeth. Don't PUSH your breath; let it come out. You should be able to get to at least 20 seconds or maybe 40 later on. Can you feel the center of your breath support getting tighter and tighter as you hiss longer? This tightness is caused by the diaphragm muscles pushing in.

Improving the projection level of your voice will not only give your message more impact but will also furnish you with a greater feeling of confidence when speaking publicly.

How to Project Your Voice

In order to make your voice carry, it must be supported by a stream of air just like a Ping-Pong ball is supported by a stream of water. Your voice also depends on a fine stream of air which is under slight pressure.

Using a loud voice without proper air support will strain your vocal cords.

When the water pipe is bent out of shape, the ball will fall to the side.

If your body is bent because of poor posture you will not be able to support your voice with enough air from your lungs. As a result of poor posture, your voice will not have any *carrying power*.

Good posture will help to support your voice more effectively. Good posture means:

(a) Stand with back straight.

(b) Place weight evenly on the balls of your feet.

(c) Keep your chest OUT.

(d) Don't raise your shoulders as you take a breath.

(e) Say a long s-s-s-s-s-s-s sound with your hand on your diaphragm. Try to keep your diaphragm muscles IN.

Take a deep breath and you will notice that your chest will get larger. Next let the air out slowly trying to keep your chest in an expanded position at the top. Try *not* to raise your shoulders as you do this.

When you let the air out, the diaphragm muscles tend to move upward and inward as shown in Illus. 1, page 6.

If you can't get this diaphragm muscle working, try grunting or making a long s-s-s-s-s sound.

To make your voice travel farther you must push HARDER with this diaphragm muscle.

Your diaphragm muscle pushes on your lungs causing air to come out under pressure.

1. Round your lips as though you were going to whistle. Wet your finger.
2. Blow a fine stream of air onto your finger and slowly move your finger to arm's length.
3. As you are blowing, put your hand on your stomach or diaphragm muscles. Your diaphragm muscles should feel like that when you are speaking to a person located 15 feet or more away from you.

If your voice is not supported by a forceful enough stream of air, your consonants will be made poorly and your voice will not be very loud or travel very far. LET THE AIR OUT SLOWLY BUT UNDER THE PRESSURE OF YOUR DIAPHRAGM MUSCLES.

This is an exercise to make your voice carry.

APPENDIX A

Recommended Materials on Ventriloquism

Bergen, Edgar—LP—"Lessons in Ventriloquism" (Juro Novelty Co., 18 East 18th St., New York, N.Y. 10003.)

Maher Ventriloquists Studios—An excellent course in ventriloquism—Studio NY-35, Box 420, Littleton, Colorado, 80120.

A condensed version of course called "Ventriloquism in a Nutshell."

Neller, Bob—"The New Way to Learn Ventriloquism"—On tape reels, cassettes, or LP's.

Nelson, Jimmy—2 LP's—"Instant Ventriloquism for Beginner"; "Ventriloquism 2"—(more advanced). (Juro Novelty Co., 18 East 18th Street, New York, N.Y. 10003.)

Stadelman, Paul—"Ventriloquism of Today" plus a reel (6" on Alpha and Omega of Ventriloquism) (can be obtained from most of above addresses.)

Winchell, Paul—"Ventriloquism for Fun and Profit"—Most of the addresses above and Micky Hades Enterprises, Box 476, Calgary, Alberta, Canada.

APPENDIX B

Glossary

Agent—The person who manages the business part of the act. A good agent will not only secure bookings for a performer but will also arrange national show tours doing all of the advance promotional work.

Beginner's Alphabet—The standard alphabet omitting the difficult sounds of B, F, M, P, V, W.

Buzz—The buzz is an extended long "eeeeee" sound that is under slight pressure from the diaphragm. This diffuse sound is the basis for the ventriloquial voice.

Coin Clip—The coin clip is a gimmick usually pinned under the jacket that can hold several 50-cent pieces. The 50-cent pieces can be secretly stolen or removed when required.

Contract—A written agreement among the agent, performer and the booker and usually includes the date, time, place and fee for an engagement.

Dialogue—A conversation that is usually between the ventriloquist's voice and the dummy's voice.

Diaphragm—A muscle dividing the rib cage and lungs from other lower body organs. By pushing on the lungs, the diaphragm helps to place the dummy voice under slight pressure.

Double-Divided Breath—The dividing of the air from your windpipe into two separate streams of air, which is also the basis of the ventriloquist voice. It is achieved by the arching of tongue and the pressure exerted by the diaphragm on the lungs.

Drone—An extended "ah" sound that is under slight pressure from the diaphragm. This diffuse sound is the basis for the ventriloquial voice.

Infantile Speech—The act of children substituting sounds in words or phrases. (*T*ome and *d*o for *C*ome and *g*o.)

Manipulation—The act of moving the dummy to make it seem endowed with lifelike actions.

Misdirection—The act of directing the attention of the spectators toward an unimportant maneuver in the magical sequence.

Miser's Dream—An effect in which coins are magically extracted from the air and dropped into a glistening metal bucket.

Muffled voice—A ventriloquial voice that is used to create the illusion that your partner is speaking from inside a suitcase or a closet.

Pantomime—Performing your vent routine with all of the actions but NO SOUND.

Situation Comedy—A comedy routine in which the laugh is obtained not by a joke or pun but by the unusual situation created.

Sound substitutions—One sound in a word is exchanged for another sound which is similar. An example would be the "be" in bottle is exchanged for the "vh" sound. A ventriloquist uses sound substitutions with words containing the B, F, M, P, V and W sounds.

Timing—The ventriloquist's ability to pace his dialogue so that the audience has time to comprehend what he is saying and at the same time he must allow a few seconds for them to react to the punch line before proceeding with his next bit.

Twentieth Century Silks—A magic routine in which a silk handkerchief vanishes only to materialize later between two previously tied ones.

Ventriloquial voice—This is the dummy's voice and it is produced by dividing the breath streams to enable more air to be directed through the nasal resonating chambers.

Ventriloquism—The art of speaking without moving the lips so that the sounds produced seem to *emanate* from another source.

Vibration—Any fast continuous back and forth movement.

Voice Contrast—The difference between the ventriloquist's voice and the dummy's voice.

APPENDIX C
Miscellaneous Madness

VENTRILOQUIST: I hear that you have enrolled in a singing course.

STANLEY: Oh yeah!, I even got second prize in the contest.

VENTRILOQUIST: Excellent! How many sang in the contest?

STANLEY: Two!

VENTRILOQUIST: How many songs did the winner sing?

STANLEY: None! When they heard me sing, they gave him the first prize!

VENTRILOQUIST: *(singing)* My song gets better as it goes along.

STANLEY: Yeah! because you are closer to the END!

VENTRILOQUIST: What are you going to sing, Stanley?

STANLEY: "Snow, Beautiful Snow."

VENTRILOQUIST: I've never heard of "Snow, Beautiful Snow."

STANLEY: You should have. There was enough of it around this year!

STANLEY: How did they invent spaghetti?

VENTRILOQUIST: I have no idea.

STANLEY: Some guy sure used his noodle?

STANLEY: What grades of eggs do you have?

VENTRILOQUIST: Second, third and fourth grades.

STANLEY: No, thanks, I want some that have graduated!

(if you get a dry throat)

VENTRILOQUIST: This collar is so tight I can hardly talk!

STANLEY: That's your shirt all right, but you've got your head through the buttonhole.

VENTRILOQUIST: Why is your January report card so poor?

STANLEY: Well, you know how things are. Things are always marked down after Christmas.

(when you get upset with your partner)
VENTRILOQUIST: Oh, you are too much!
STANLEY: Oh no! I'm just enough.

VENTRILOQUIST: How come you were running when I saw you last night?
STANLEY: I was stopping a fight.
VENTRILOQUIST: How could you be stopping a fight?
STANLEY: It was between me and another guy.

VENTRILOQUIST: Why were you sticking your tongue out?
STANLEY: What else would you do if a guy was strangling you?

(to a heckler)
STANLEY: Say, they've got the wrong guy in the suitcase!

(if you forget a line)
VENTRILOQUIST: I'm getting so bad I don't know if I'm coming or going.
STANLEY: It really doesn't matter. You don't look good either way!

(if you mix up your lines)
STANLEY: Well, I guess that's what I get for studying my script in the dark.
VENTRILOQUIST: Why in the world did you study your script in the dark?
STANLEY: Well, it's restful on the eyes!

VENTRILOQUIST: Did your mother help you with this problem?
STANLEY: No, I got it wrong all by myself.

(ventriloquist singing)
STANLEY: Can you carry a tune?
VENTRILOQUIST: Most certainly.
STANLEY: Well, why don't you carry the one you're whistling out to the back yard and bury it.

NOTE: Never copy a joke or dialogue word for word, as the end routine will sound stilted. Every joke or gag should be adapted to match your and your partner's personalities. If you avoid wordy build-ups and keep your punch lines short, simple and tightly spaced, the comedy will have more impact upon the audience. Build-up lines that are repeated or said more loudly or slowly tend to reinforce the laugh-eliciting ability of the punch line.

APPENDIX D

Suppliers of Dummies

Finis and Company,
624 West 3rd
Waterloo, Iowa, 50701

Hades Enterprises,
Box 476,
Calgary, Alberta, Canada

Juro Celebrity Dolls,
18 East 18th Street,
New York, New York, 10003

Maher Ventriloquists Studios,
Studio NV-35, Box 420,
Littleton, Colorado 80120

Tannen Magic Ltd.,
1540 Broadway,
New York, N.Y. 10036

Index